An ABC Manager's Primer

Straight Talk on Activity-Based Costing

by

Gary Cokins

Alan Stratton, CMA

Jack Helbling

IRWIN

Professional Publishing

Burr Ridge, Illinois
New York, New York

A project undertaken by the
Institute of Management Accountants
Montvale, New Jersey
Consortium for Advanced Manufacturing-International/Cost Management Systems
(formerly Computer Aided Manufacturing-International)
Arlington, Texas

The ABC Cross

	Resources [*What is used to do work*]	
Cost Drivers [*Why work is done*]	Activities [*Work*]	Performance Measures [*How well work is done*]
	Objects of Work [*To what, or for whom work is done*]	

Scripted text translates activity-based costing into information about work. Each type of information in the ABC cross has a defined role in the continuous improvement process. The ABC cross was conceived by Peter B.B. Turney and Norman Raffish. In its original form, it was published by CAM-I in March 1991. This new view was introduced to CMS sponsors by Cost Technology, Inc. in San Diego on March 9, 1993.

Published by
Institute of Management Accountants
10 Paragon Drive
Montvale, NJ 07645-1760

Claire Barth, Editor

This book is dedicated to

the late Robert A. Bonsack

a craftsman in the field of advanced cost management.

—————————————————

Foreword

IMA frequently provides practitioners, academics, and students with case studies, seminars, and training aids on activity-based costing (ABC) and prides itself on being the premier resource on the subject. *An ABC Manager's Primer,* written with a clear, informed understanding of what ABC is all about, is based on real implementation experiences. In this guide, as in *Implementing Activity-Based Cost Management: Moving from Analysis to Action*, also published by IMA, the essence of ABC/ABM comes through. Although critics question the importance of ABC/ABM in driving behavioral changes within an organization, in this primer the concepts are well articulated, so that managers will be encouraged to start an implementation initiative. At least, there are enough success stories to justify the cost of probing further.

The three Rs now revitalizing the way business is conducted in the United States are reengineering, reinventing, and redesigning processes. *An ABC Manager's Primer* offers an easy way to find out what's going on in this area. Readers should focus on Figures 2-8 and 2-12 and read the whole of Section 4—the key to understanding ABC/ABM. Benchmarking metrics referred to in Section 5 are expected to be readily accessible to organizations participating in IMA's Continuous Improvement Center (CIC). In the final analysis, ABC/ABM will facilitate processes that are effective, efficient, and robust. This primer will provide guidance on the journey.

IMA recognizes the contribution of CAM-I's CMS program to the management accounting literature. IMA has participated in CAM-I since its inception and is collaborating actively on common study themes. The management accounting profession is indebted to Peter Zampino of CAM-I/CMS, to the primer's authors, and to IMA's 1992-93 Committee on Research, chaired by Dennis Neider, CMA, for making this book possible.

This guide reflects the views of the authors and not necessarily those of IMA or the Committee on Research.

Julian Freedman
Director of Research
Institute of Management Accountants

Preface

When operations personnel, engineers, or managers are asked how well their organization's accounting information serves them and their coworkers, the answer is rarely flattering. Why? Typically, accounting systems satisfy external reporting requirements and some executive management tastes, but they usually fall short in helping managers detect problems or their solutions. Traditional accounting systems simply are not designed to deliver managerial information.

Activity-based information significantly boosts the value and utility of financial data for decision makers and empowered employees. People can relate to activity-based data. Users of the data routinely remark that it is common sense.

This primer addresses a lack of awareness of what activity-based costing (ABC) is and is not. This lack of awareness is an impediment to change. The remedies are either to attend seminars, buy lengthy textbooks, or read articles on the subject. Too often, however, the books never get read or attendees return from seminars enlightened but without the capability to act or get started.

An ABC Manager's Primer is meant to be a quick read. Everyone's time is valuable. The book has three levels of detail. If you want to skip the reading, then look at the pictures. The second level is the text in larger type. The indented paragraphs in smaller type provide the third, more detailed level.

This guide is written with short, to-the-point sentences and assumes readers are moderately informed about their organization's existing (and flawed) costing practices. Ideally, readers are members of a project team, or sponsors, or will receive the benefit of activity-based costing or an activity analysis assignment. The book is intended to take the mystique out of activity-based costing. It is not written as a how-to-implement cookbook, but it will give a head start for action. The three authors have led multiple ABC projects, and the lessons they have learned are revealed in this collaborative effort.

We would like to acknowledge the support and encouragement of Peter Zampino, director of Advanced Management Programs, CAM-I; Julian Freedman, director of research, Institute of Management Accountants (IMA); and the sponsoring companies of the CMS Program.

About the Authors

Gary Cokins

Gary Cokins is a principal consultant with EDS and leads its center of expertise for financial and cost management systems. His services include the integration of activity-based measurement with time-based, quality-based, and cost-based systems to support customer-directed business processes.

Prior to joining EDS, he was a senior manager for both KPMG Peat Marwick and Deloitte, Haskins & Sells. His focus at both firms was reforming cost management practices for clients to align with business strategies and to support cycle time-based engineering and materials management. He worked 10 years for FMC Corporation as both a division controller and materials manager.

Mr. Cokins graduated with honors from Cornell University in industrial engineering and has an MBA from Northwestern University's Kellogg School of Management. He is certified in the theory of constraints (TOC) and is Certified in Production and Inventory Management (CPIM) by the American Production and Inventory Control Society (APICS). In 1992, he was honored with CAM-I's Award for Distinguished Achievement in Cost Management.

Alan Stratton, CMA

Alan Stratton, vice president of Cost Technology, Inc. has more than 18 years experience directing accounting functions and developing both personal computer and mainframe systems.

Formerly, Mr. Stratton led National Semiconductor's (NSC) activity-based management implementation. He led site implementations and developed training and systems to support the implementation of ABM worldwide within NSC. Previously, he was the controller for a NSC manufacturing operation and has held responsible finance and cost management positions at Atari, General Instruments, GTE, and Arthur Andersen.

Mr. Stratton graduated summa cum laude from Brigham Young University and has a master's degree in accountancy from Brigham Young University. He is a CMA and earned a silver medal for exam performance. He is also a CPA and earned honorable mention for CPA exam performance. In 1992 he was honored with CAM-I's Award for Distinguished Achievement in Cost Management.

Jack Helbling

Jack Helbling has been managing the development and use of activity-based cost management at Procter & Gamble (P&G) for the last three years. Prior to his current assignment, he had various manufacturing, industrial engineering, and accounting assignments at P&G, including (operating) department manager and plant financial manager.

Mr. Helbling has a bachelor of science degree in industrial engineering from Penn State University.

Table of Contents

1. The Rise of Activity-Based Costing (ABC)

What Is ABC?

ABC is a simple concept, yet implementers and users frequently find it complicated. Perhaps too many articles and seminars have stressed ABC accomplishments or benefits but have given too little information that explained what it actually is. This guide is intended to eliminate the mystique from ABC.

First—ABC is only data, but someone must use the data effectively and creatively or the whole project is a waste of time. Although ABC is only data, it can be very powerful and spark project teams or decision makers to take new steps or draw innovative conclusions. In the sense described above, ABC is part of change management. ABC is also an enabler for continuous improvement and decision support. It makes tools such as just-in-time (JIT), total quality management (TQM), and business process reengineering (BPR) more effective.

ABC is currently not a financial reporting system designed to serve regulatory agencies such as the Internal Revenue Service or Securities Exchange Commission, but it will be in the future. ABC provides managerial information in financial metric form. Financial denominations, such as U.S. dollars, serve as measures for the language of business. ABC communicates dollars to nonfinancial managers better than traditional cost accounting does, because ABC physically mirrors the activities of people, machines, and equipment.

ABC communicates to people the rate at which activities consume resources as well as why the resources are used. People need to use common sense in implementing ABC's clear, relevant data, and then their understanding of the data will be enhanced; thus, ABC creates benefits.

Why ABC Is Becoming Popular

Like JIT, ABC was described by accountants in the 1800s and early 1900s. Today, it is commonly remarked that the new managerial techniques are simply a repackaging of old techniques. This

Figure 1-1.
CURRENT BUSINESS
ENVIRONMENT

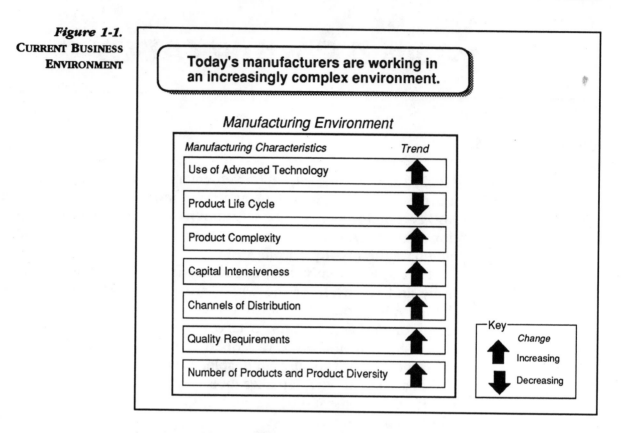

comment is generally true in regard to ABC. Although the basic mechanics of ABC are simple, the nature of what is costed—namely, products and processes—is changing. As shown in Figure 1-1, complexity, variety, and diversity in businesses have escalated dramatically. An increasingly complex business environment leads to higher overhead costs—complexity breeds overhead.

The manner of conducting business has shifted from the past, but costing practices have not correspondingly shifted enough. Consequently, valuations of product costs are grossly distorted and managerial accounting information is inadequate. ABC simply brings cost information to the level needed so managers can make decisions and gain a competitive edge in the current business environment.

As businesses have become more complex, the elements of cost have shifted and become more mixed, as shown in Figure 1-2. Overhead costs are replacing the direct costs of touch-laborers and purchased materials. These overhead costs are, in reality, technology and people who sustain productivity gains and manage complexity.

The overhead or indirect costs typically are controlled today by using responsibility cost center budgeting. Budget controls are becoming less effective for managing businesses, however, because of growing dependencies among departments and functions. Departments and functions are being ridiculed as organizational silos and stovepipes. Budget variance management at the account line-item level has always been controversial as a method of control. Good performers are either good negotiators at budget creation time or they know just how to shift the charges and credits between accounts. There is gamesmanship to budgeting.

In the last 10 years, the cross-functional behavior within businesses has become much more recognized and appreciated. Department walls are coming down, and there is less throwing-the-order-over-the-wall behavior. Managers are rising collectively above their walls and taking account of the interconnectivity and mutual dependencies among their departments.

Responsibility cost center budgets lose effectiveness as this internal supplier-customer chain is followed. For example, when a purchasing agent saves a dollar by buying a substandard product, other downstream departments will make up for it in rework, overtime, or quality or in another nonvalue-added activity.

ABC is not old wine (data) in a new bottle (revolutionary accounting). It is new wine from an old bottle. The event that has caused the change is the introduction of the computer. Relational databases and fourth generation languages now allow the rapid reorganization of data. The proliferation in mix, variety, complexity, and diversity, as well as the displacement of direct labor and material costs by overhead, has overwhelmed traditional cost accounting practices. Without ABC, executives and managers are forced into a guessing game about what things really cost.

Figure 1-2.
KEY PRINCIPLES
OF ABC

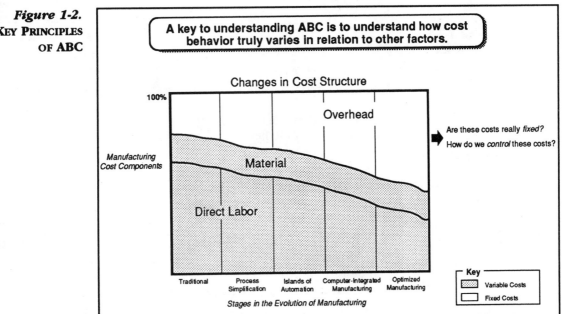

The Multiple Uses for ABC

From a historical perspective, ABC was used first to describe improved product costing. Professors Robert S. Kaplan and Robin Cooper of the Harvard Business School (Cooper is now at Claremont Graduate School, Claremont, California) became leading spokesmen by articulating in business periodicals how grotesque misallocations of overhead could distort the true costs of products. In conventional systems, direct labor stated in hours or dollars has been relied on as the basis for assigning overhead costs to products.

Kaplan and Cooper noted, as did engineers and product managers, that significant amounts of overhead activities, from testing to material handling, are disproportionately consumed by certain parts, products, and product families. Traditional burden-averaging and labor-based cost systems do not capture the disproportion. Today's cost accounting systems do not mirror the true economics of physical production and resource cost consumption. ABC provides a closer match between costs and output.

ABC corrects the distortions so that people can know what processes, services, and products truly cost. In addition, ABC includes costs well beyond those used to compute inventory costs, for example, selling and distribution expenses. ABC has no readily identifiable boundaries because it is a managerial system and therefore its characteristics depend on how it will be used. ABC can provide "total delivered cost" information.

Pioneering companies, such as Hewlett-Packard, became early ABC implementers by launching experimental pilot ABC models. As time passed, practitioners learned ABC's capabilities, gained ABC experience, and expanded ABC applications. ABC has evolved into activity-based management (ABM), a more encompassing term, and includes the managing of costs as well as a more proper assignment of costs to processes and products.

In this primer, ABC is the tool that identi-

Figure 1-3.
WHAT IS ABC?

Definition of Activity-Based Costing

- A method that measures the cost and performance of process-related activities and cost objects

- Assigns cost activities based on their use of resources, and assigns cost to cost objects, such as products or customers, based on their use of activities

- Recognizes the causal relationship of cost drivers to activities

Source: *The CAM-I Glossary of Activity-Based Management*, 1990

Figure 1-4.
WHAT IS ABM?

> **Definition of Activity-Based Management**
>
> - A discipline focusing on the management of activities as the route to continuously improve both the value received by customers and the profit earned by providing this value
>
> - Includes cost-driver analysis, activity analysis, and performance analysis
>
> - Draws on activity-based costing as a major source for data and information
>
> Source: *The CAM-I Glossary of Activity-Based Management*, 1990

fies and computes costs for activities, processes, and outputs of activities, such as products or services. Figure 1-3 shows the definition used by CAM-I (Consortium for Advanced Manufacturing-International; formerly Computer Aided Manufacturing-International).

ABM, on the other hand, provides information for managing activities using ABC data and other tools to achieve continuous improvement (see Figure 1-4 for the definition of ABM).

In the following pages, ABM is introduced as a method not only for reporting costs but also for managing them. However, do not equate managing with controlling. ABC/ABM data are used far more for predictive modeling than for control. Today, cost data for purposes of control have been eclipsed by faster feedback from total quality management, such as statistical process control practices, or from real-time, integrated information systems.

Why Activity-Based Management?

Why use activity-based management in addition to activity-based costing? With ABM data, teams are empowered to reengineer business processes, to identify waste, to reduce cycle times, and to accomplish these tasks profitably. These improvements are achieved by providing activity-based metrics that traditional accounting cannot provide. Figure 1-5 shows that ABM gives data users the opportunity to receive and use relevant information. It provides them with a chance to add significant value to the management process.

Companies are walking on thin ice if they believe their cost numbers from a traditional system. Generally, managers are under an illusion that if the accountants can produce the numbers, the system must be working. They are confusing information systems with costing practices.

❖ ❖ ❖ ❖ ❖

ABC/ABM can be implemented in service businesses as well as in discrete, job shop, and process manufacturing businesses. To date,

Figure 1-5.
WHY USE ABM?

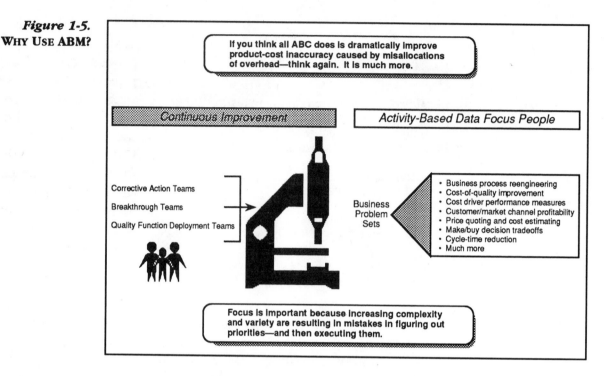

If you think all ABC does is dramatically improve product-cost inaccuracy caused by misallocations of overhead—think again. It is much more.

Continuous Improvement

Activity-Based Data Focus People

Corrective Action Teams

Breakthrough Teams

Quality Function Deployment Teams

Business Problem Sets

• Business process reengineering
• Cost-of-quality improvement
• Cost driver performance measures
• Customer/market channel profitability
• Price quoting and cost estimating
• Make/buy decision tradeoffs
• Cycle-time reduction
• Much more

Focus is important because increasing complexity and variety are resulting in mistakes in figuring out priorities—and then executing them.

most implementations have been in manufacturing environments. However, service businesses also can realize significant benefits by understanding how cost behavior relates to business requirements. Service providers such as banks and insurance companies increasingly are deploying ABC/ABM.[1]

❖ ❖ ❖ ❖ ❖

How costly is it to implement and maintain an ABC/ABM system? Do the benefits exceed the costs? Is the view worth the climb? The answer predictably is "it depends." Because there is so much freedom and flexibility in designing an ABC/ABM system, it makes sense to keep the system simple initially and minimize the time and effort spent in collecting and calculating the data. Use shortcuts and workarounds. Estimates in ABC/ABM stand the credibility test because cost materiality and relevance are considered in the design phase. Further, Pareto's law whereby "few account for many" prevails in understanding cost behavior.

Section 2 relates how the assignment of costs is distorted and flawed. Understanding how to correct for errors of "misallocation" exposes the framework used in Section 3 and throughout the rest of the *ABC Manager's Primer*. Sections 3 through 7 focus on performance improvement.

---

[1]If you want to read fast, you can skip the paragraphs in small type.

2. How ABC Systems Are Built

The Importance of Understanding ABC Design

Make no mistake about this next point. When ABC pilots are successful, the primary reason is because the pilots were designed so that the ABM data would be useful to operations personnel. The product costing data fall out as extra bonus information.

The explanation for this situation is behavioral. When operational people are involved initially in revamping the enterprise's cost practices and cost system, the new system reflects their needs. They buy in and sustain its use. They like the new cost data to be reliably reported at timely intervals. If the accounting personnel revamp the system, operations personnel will perceive the event as just another meaningless financial exercise. Remember, it is easier to implement ABC than it is to sustain it.

Regardless of who you are and what you may do with ABC/ABM data, it is critical for you to understand how an ABC/ABM system is constructed. You do not *buy* an ABC/ABM system and plug it in. Like other programs, it is a process. But an ABC/ABM system is more tangible, with hard data resulting from its design.

It is easier to learn how ABM works by first learning how ABC works. Consequently, the remainder of this section is, in effect, what action-oriented operations personnel might call an instruction manual for constructing product costs. But this section is much more. It explains the underlying principles of costing that apply universally for both valuing and managing products and processes.

ABC/ABM is not strictly about costs. It is about resource use and consumption. In this section, we learn how costs are traced and assigned based on cause-and-effect behavior and relationships with cost drivers. Granted, this section simply *reslices* overhead costs. In Section 3, we discuss how companies reduce overhead by *managing* costs.

The ABC/ABM Framework

ABC design focuses first on activities. Activities are what people and equipment do to satisfy customer needs. Activities are the thing that consumes business resources. The lack of an effective activity-based focus would make ABC just another cost accounting system. By focusing on activities instead of on departments or functions, ABC makes it possible for ABM to be a powerful tool for managing, understanding, and, most important, improving a business.

Figure 2-1.
ABC MODEL

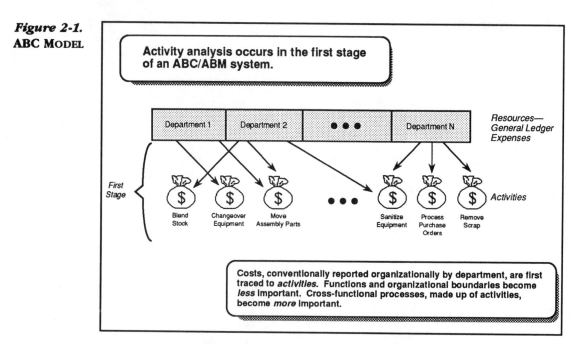

The ABC model in Figure 2-1 is similar to a pump, valve, and pipe system—costs are pumped to activities using special and sensitive valves. All resource consumption, represented by general ledger costs, is first accumulated in the general ledger using conventional business systems such as payroll, accounts payable, journal entries, and so forth. In the process of determining activity costs, all resource costs are transferred through the pipes into activity costs.

❖ ❖ ❖ ❖ ❖

Resource costs represent people, computers, technology, equipment, machines, supplies, tooling, and other factors. These factors allow productive activity and the serving of customers, whether internal or external.

❖ ❖ ❖ ❖ ❖

Because ABC/ABM focuses on activities, its activity-based reports are more informative than traditional month-end department or cost center statements produced by the general ledger. As shown in Figure 2-2, activity costs accurately mirror what an organization does—for better or for worse. Activities are custom defined when a team designs the ABC system.

Activities are best defined using an active verb and object convention. For example, "create labor routings." Managers and employees relate to costs described in this manner because they know they can change or affect an activity that is performed by a person or a machine. In some cases, they may choose to eliminate the activity.

❖ ❖ ❖ ❖ ❖

After enough practice, custom-defined systems within a company can be supported by standard activity definitions using an activity dictionary. However, the initial learning experience (build from scratch) is important and valuable for project team members.

❖ ❖ ❖ ❖ ❖

The weakness of traditional general ledger reports is that expenses are reported by department and spending account. General ledger reports describe only *what* is spent, while activities describe *how* it is spent. When managers review their monthly budget variance reports from the general ledger, they are either happy or sad but not necessarily any smarter! ABC fixes this.

After defining activities and computing activity costs, the implementer distributes costs again. This time, activity costs are distributed to the cost object that uses the activity. Cost objects are usually parts, services, ingredients, products, customers, or distribu-

Figure 2-2.
ABC's INFORMATIVE
REPORT

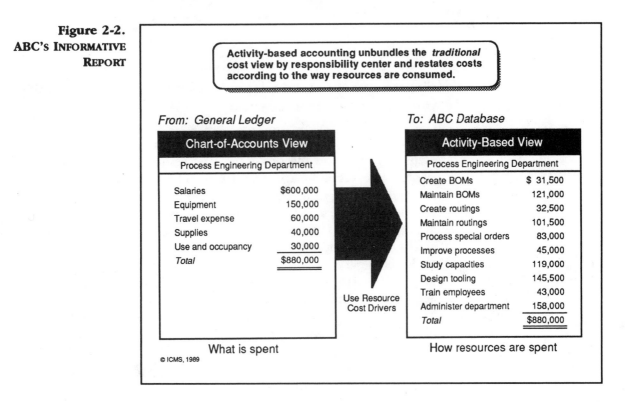

Activity-based accounting unbundles the *traditional* cost view by responsibility center and restates costs according to the way resources are consumed.

From: General Ledger

Chart-of-Accounts View

Process Engineering Department

Salaries	$600,000
Equipment	150,000
Travel expense	60,000
Supplies	40,000
Use and occupancy	30,000
Total	$880,000

What is spent

Use Resource
Cost Drivers

To: ABC Database

Activity-Based View

Process Engineering Department

Create BOMs	$ 31,500
Maintain BOMs	121,000
Create routings	32,500
Maintain routings	101,500
Process special orders	83,000
Improve processes	45,000
Study capacities	119,000
Design tooling	145,500
Train employees	43,000
Administer department	158,000
Total	$880,000

How resources are spent

tion channels. Activity cost drivers recognize the proportionate discharge of each activity cost into its cost objects. Well-designed ABC systems remove skewed cost distributions by minimizing the overhead averaging so prevalent in today's allocation-based designs.

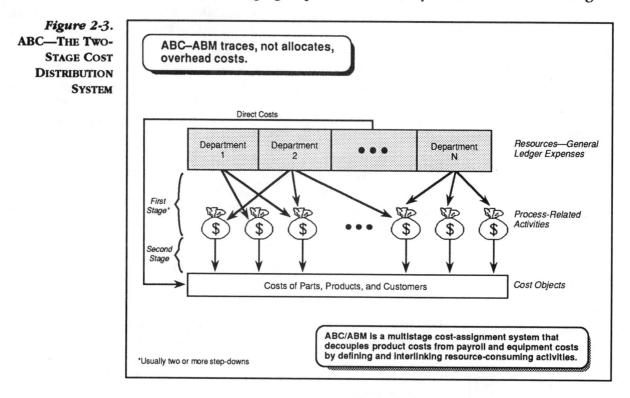

Figure 2-3.
ABC—THE TWO-STAGE COST DISTRIBUTION SYSTEM

As shown in Figure 2-3, activity-based costing is a two-stage cost distribution system. Products and customers consume activities. Activities consume resource costs.

❖ ❖ ❖ ❖ ❖

Advanced ABC/ABM implementers recognize that multiple steps can make up the first-stage cost assignment, the resource drivers (the second-stage cost assignment uses activity drivers). After general ledger resource costs are unbundled and accumulated into activities, additional optional steps are to redistribute the activity costs into macro activities or processes. For example, the activity "unscheduled machine repair" may draw resources from multiple departments. This activity cost might be an intermediate step to be combined with similar activities to feed the macro activity of the machine, such as "drill holes." This process is the "step-down allocation," but with ABC it is accomplished at the activity level, not percent-of-department, a critical distinction.

❖ ❖ ❖ ❖ ❖

Ideally, all costs could be charged directly to activities and then be assigned directly to end products. However, the cost and complexity of data collection can exceed the value of the improved information. In addition, most overhead costs are difficult, if not impossible, to charge directly to cost objects. Traditional cost accounting arbitrarily allocates nondirect overhead costs, a method that corrupts cost integrity. To ABC/ABM, allocation is a dirty word. ABC/ABM resolves misallocations by using resource and activity drivers that reflect unique consumption patterns and link cause and effect to the cost-assignment process (see Figure 2-4).

Figure 2-4.
ABC Improves Upon Traditional Costing

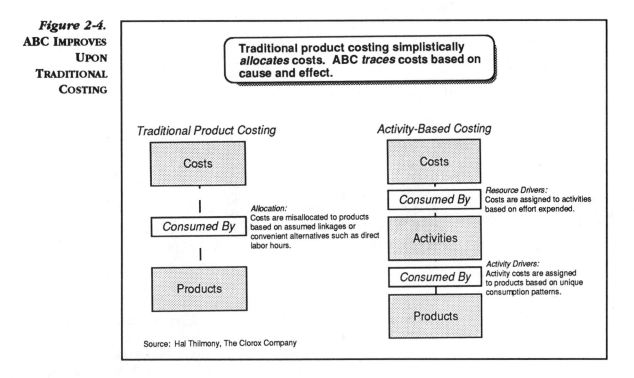

> Traditional product costing simplistically *allocates* costs. ABC *traces* costs based on cause and effect.

Traditional Product Costing

Costs

|
Consumed By
|

Products

Allocation:
Costs are misallocated to products based on assumed linkages or convenient alternatives such as direct labor hours.

Activity-Based Costing

Costs

Consumed By

Activities

Consumed By

Products

Resource Drivers:
Costs are assigned to activities based on effort expended.

Activity Drivers:
Activity costs are assigned to products based on unique consumption patterns.

Source: Hal Thilmony, The Clorox Company

❖ ❖ ❖ ❖ ❖

Misallocation occurs because the variability of indirect and overhead costs is not always in proportion to the allocation base. For example, distributing the cost of buyers in the purchasing department based on labor or machine hours makes little sense. Instead, ABC/ABM would use the number of purchase orders or another measure that links the consumption of the costs of procurement activities more directly to those parts and products that place demands on those activities.

❖ ❖ ❖ ❖ ❖

Figure 2-5 shows that in ABC, direct material costs are attached to products using a bill of materials (BOM) or a formula. Similarly, direct labor costs may be attached using a routing bill of labor. Despite the direct attachment of material and labor costs, many resource costs remain as indirect or overhead costs.

Figure 2-5.
ABC/ABM
Model—Cost-
Assignment View

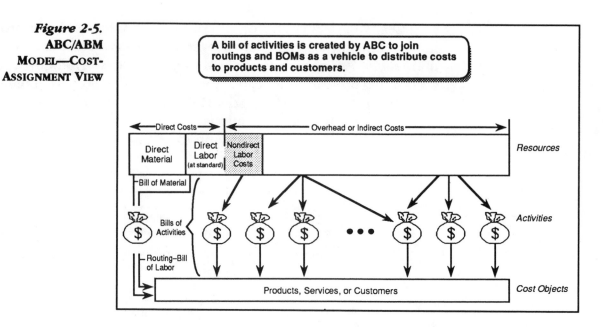

ABC attaches indirect costs in a logical way to the consumers of these costs, using cause-and-effect reasoning. First, ABC links resource costs to activities based on effort expended or material consumed. ABC then uses activity drivers to attach indirect activity costs to cost objects in proportion to their consumption by the cost objects. Using a bill of activities makes it easier to understand the true cost of the cost object.

❖ ❖ ❖ ❖ ❖

In job shop or custom manufacturing businesses that have fewer repetitive end-items, laborers and engineers might complete a work order or project accounting input form that serves as a direct labor cost tool. ABC's two-stage distribution scheme is used to trace the remaining indirect costs to the areas that consume them.

❖ ❖ ❖ ❖ ❖

ABC's additional bill of activities serves, in effect, as a proxy direct-bill charge. An ABC bill of activities charge is less precise than a direct charge, but, on the other hand, it is far superior to using allocations that have little or no correlation to the way costs are consumed. The defect of traditional cost systems is that allocations do not correlate with the resources they supposedly are consuming. ABC removes such distortions. The task for ABC project teams is to shift the cost assignment path from right to left as shown in Figure 2-6.

❖ ❖ ❖ ❖ ❖

To date, many companies use ABC only to perform product costing. Some companies use ABC to determine costs consumed to serve different customers. In this case, the mix of customer services, not products, causes a significant portion of overhead costs. These costs are not consumed proportionately by activities for different customers in relation to sales or margins. Customers with large sales are not necessarily profitable to a supplier. ABC makes it easy to align customer costs with profits or losses.

❖ ❖ ❖ ❖ ❖

First-time observers of ABC have a nightmare of having to collect and edit astronomical amounts of data. The next sections eliminate these fears. With ABC, closeness is better than precision.

Tools for Information Collection

Resource cost drivers are an innovative concept in ABC modeling. In traditional systems, financial controllers usually create elaborate, step-down, sequential allocations that distribute service department cost to production work centers based on percentage estimates. These allocations are often flawed because they assume arbitrary relationships, for example, using square feet or head count. These measures do not reflect disproportionate resource consumption. Such burden-averaging techniques are convenient for accountants but are not of service to users of information.

With ABC, resource cost drivers replace the step-down allocations with cause-and-effect relationships at the activity level, not at the departmental level. Figure 2-7 shows that resource drivers are reasonable estimates of time, effort, or cost and often are obtained through interviews. In some cases, labor reporting systems and

Figure 2-6.
ABC REMOVES
DISTORTIONS

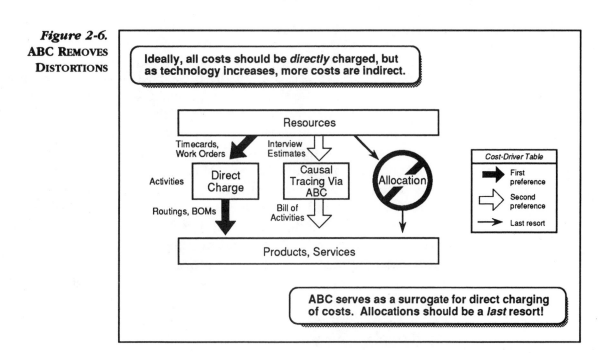

Figure 2-7.
ABC/ABM DATA
COLLECTION

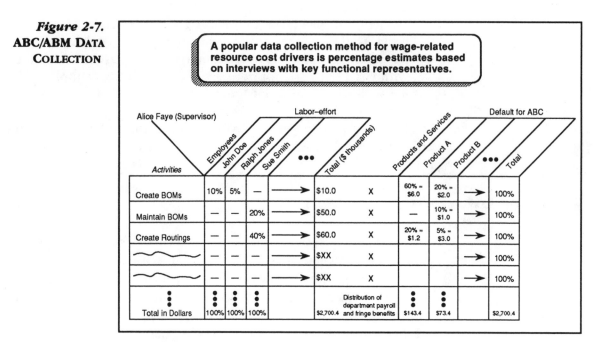

work order systems, for example those used by maintenance departments, are additional sources of data.

❖ ❖ ❖ ❖ ❖

Interviews and survey forms are not the only source for estimating resource drivers, but they are the most common one. Additional tools for data collection include:

- Observation,
- Timekeeping systems,
- Questionnaires,
- Storyboards.

❖ ❖ ❖ ❖ ❖

ABC activities are defined in physical terms, such as moving scrap. ABC users like these terms because they help them to relate to an action and to understand what object receives or benefits from the stated action.

Today, few companies use ABC to generate a monthly accounting statement or variance report. Many companies use a representative time period under normal operating conditions, such as a fiscal quarter or one year. In these cases, ABC is a static snapshot of a time period—the length of the time is analogous to a camera's film exposure. If the mix of activities and their content change quickly, ABC snapshots should be taken more frequently.

If managers want a dynamic picture of actual costs for controlling activities and evaluating performance, they should refer not only to accounting data. They should use metrics that encompass and combine measures for quality, time, and costs, but they should

Figure 2-8.
PROCESSES HAVE
THREE MEASURES

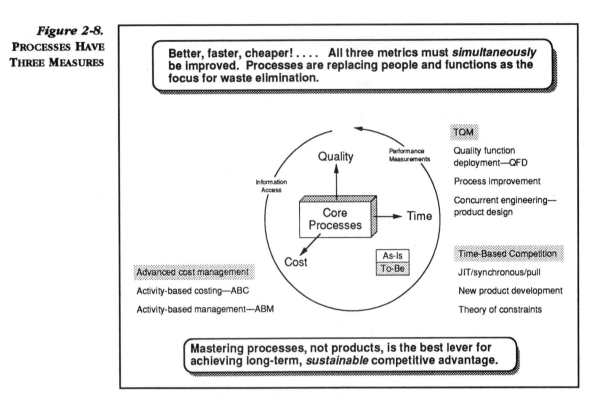

never examine any one of these metrics in isolation. Figure 2-8 reveals how companies can be "better, faster, and cheaper" by leveraging financial and nonfinancial data. Ultimately, performance measures combined with an enforced accountability for them is what really matters. You get what you measure. What is measured gets done. ABC/ABM assists in pruning dysfunctional measures and aligning the reformed measures with goals and strategies.

Timely and meaningful feedback to employees is critical to the management of activities and processes. If necessary, ABC/ABM can generate a monthly income statement analysis. However, this analysis should occur well after the off-line ABC/ABM model has been accepted as a tool. The employees should view ABC/ABM as a predictive cost planning tool and not as a control tool.

The next topic of discussion is how to define and structure the cost-assignment parameters and features, which concentrate on achieving more accurate product costing. Process costing is involved, but it will be covered in detail in Section 3.

Defining ABC/ABM to Satisfy Requirements

The first step in determining activity cost is to use the resource cost drivers to distribute factory overhead costs and other product logistics and selling costs into activities. A simple way to distribute

Figure 2-9.
ABC/ABM ACTIVITY
MECHANICS

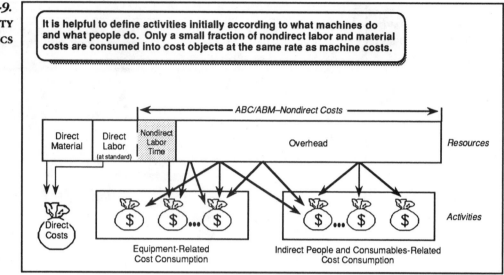

overhead resource costs to products is to imagine two separate broad routes. One route traces resource costs to equipment-related activities. The other route traces nonequipment-related, or people, activities. Figure 2-9 shows the importance of dividing activities according to what machines do and what people do.

Equipment-related activities usually are associated with technology and usually include unrecoverable (sunk) costs, as well as utility and energy costs. The maintenance and repair costs of engineers often are included, as well as specialized, indirect support costs. Equipment-related activities represent technology-related resource consumption, such as depreciation expenses.

An exception occurs when specialized, indirect people support an equipment-related activity. Equipment-related activity costs are traced to cost objects, such as parts or products, using activity drivers that have the same cost behavior characteristics as the activity. They are usually unit-volume based, such as labor hours, machine hours, or units produced.

Nonequipment-related activities, such as material handling and order processing, are usually indirect and people-effort intensive. These costs are traced to cost objects using activity drivers that likely have a step function, such as material-handling batch loads or equipment setups. Most of these costs do not vary one-for-one with unit-volume outputs or machine hours. They are, rather, the result of quantity-insensitive batches of great diversity, such as the number of products, vendors, and engineering change notices (ECNs) assocdiated with the cost object. Many of these overhead costs, such as a product family manager's salary, are exclusive to only a subset of the cost objects. Traditional cost systems spread these costs across all cost objects—ABC does not. In general, product complexity and variety cause nonequipment-related overhead in the form of people, the most flexible resource.

In addition to direct product-conversion work, the laborers classified as direct labor perform a variety of indirect tasks, such as material handling, for a surprisingly large portion of their work. These costs are more likely to be nonequipment related. Direct laborers' indirect activities should be distributed to cost objects in the same manner as activities of employees classified as indirect laborers are distributed to cost objects.

ABC does not recognize any manner of class distinction—employees are employees, and their resources are consumed. ABC does not recognize employees as being either direct or indirect. Now that overhead costs have been recast as activity costs, ABC in addition must recast activity costs into those cost objects, such as products, that uniquely consume them.

Figure 2-10.
ABC/ABM Cost Object Mechanics

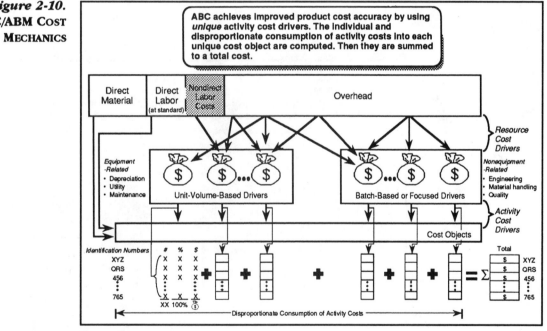

The bottom of Figure 2-10 shows how the ABC method calculates the distribution of each activity cost for the measurable consumption of each activity cost driver by each cost object. In the final step, these elements of overhead cost for each cost object are summed across. For assembled items, these component part costs are rolled up through the product structure to give the total product cost. Powerful ABC software is currently commercially available (see Appendix). This software uses relational database technology to provide a reverse audit trail that reports the sources of all costs. In addition, database technology allows the attribute data described in Section 4 to accompany the activity cost information.

✦ ✦ ✦ ✦ ✦

In reality, dividing resource costs into two categories is artificial. There are many ways to organize activity costs. However, the division of resource costs aids the design team in keeping the model accurate and relevant. Companies with low direct-labor content and high equipment costs can substitute part features (for example, number of holes) for the traditional time-based activity cost driver. These data represent design for manufacturability (DFM) information that helps design engineers achieve target costs.

✦ ✦ ✦ ✦ ✦

It is now understandable how traditional allocation practices actually misallocate costs. Why the misallocation occurs is explained in the next section (based on published research by Robin Cooper).[1]

Figure 2-11.
ABC Reflects Variable and Intensive Behavior

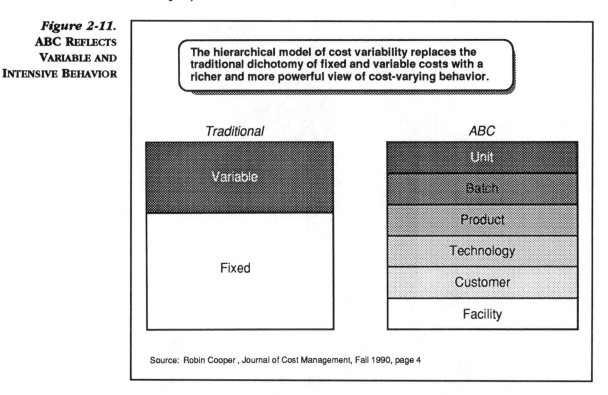

The hierarchical model of cost variability replaces the traditional dichotomy of fixed and variable costs with a richer and more powerful view of cost-varying behavior.

Traditional

Variable

Fixed

ABC

Unit

Batch

Product

Technology

Customer

Facility

Source: Robin Cooper, Journal of Cost Management, Fall 1990, page 4

---

[1] "Cost Classification in Unit-Based and Activity-Based Manufacturing Cost Systems," *Journal of Cost Management*, Fall 1990, pp. 4-14.

Maintaining Congruency

As can be seen in Figure 2-11, traditional cost systems view costs as a dichotomy of either fixed or variable costs and often are criticized for spreading the fixed, indirect costs heavily across products. Traditional cost systems allocate large overhead cost pools assuming the allocation base, such as direct labor hours, varies exactly with or reflects the degree to which those resources are consumed. ABC expands an assumed homogeneously behaving cost pool into multiple smaller heterogeneous cost pools, each with its own unique activity cost driver (for example, allocation base). With ABC, the heterogeneous cost pools and their activity drivers have similar parallel behavior.

Figure 2-12. THE HIERARCHICAL MODEL OF COST VARIABILITY

> Activity-based costing employs both unit and nonunit volume-based cost drivers.

Driver Trait		Level of Activity	Description	Examples of Activities
Variable		Unit Volume	Performed every time a unit is produced	• Drilling a hole • Supplying electricity
Nonunit Variable		Batch-Related	Performed every time a batch is produced	• Setting up a machine • Moving a batch • Ordering a purchased part
Disproportionate	To Products	Product-Sustaining	Performed to enable a product to be produced	• Engineering a product • Marketing a product
	To Processes	Technology-Sustaining	Performed to enable a technology to produce a product	• Maintaining a machine • Attending a course
	To Markets	Customer-Sustaining	Performed to service customers and prospects	• Delivering a product • Resolving complaints
Fixed; Discretionary		Facility-Sustaining	Performed to enable production to occur	• Lighting the factory • Using janitorial services • Paying rent, insurance, taxes

Source: Robin Cooper, Journal of Cost Management, Fall 1990, Page 4

As Figure 2-12 shows, an ABC design team must recognize activity differences and activity-consumption differences. The team also must avoid combining activities from different levels of the variable and cost-intensive activity hierarchy, for example, combining unit-level activities and batch-level activities. If the team traces an activity to a cost object using an incongruent activity driver, the team is still spreading costs the traditional way and is continuing to introduce distortion error.

Note that the lowest category of the hierarchy—facility-sustaining activities—is extremely insensitive to changes in unit or batch variability or in the mix of cost-intensive activities. In effect, it is clear that cost objects do not cause these costs to occur! We recognize them as those fixed costs (or highly discretionary costs) that are inevitable and ultimately to be recovered with volume, any volume.

There is a subtle difference between support costs and staff costs. Support departments exist to serve other departments, including the direct line-based departments. Staff departments perform administrative duties and would be classified as facility-sustaining. Section 4 covers the controversies from full-absorption costing.

Profit Distortions from Traditional Cost Systems

Markets increasingly are being segmented into smaller units, which are addressed separately, with their own desired product and service variations. Although production managers would like a trend reversal back toward standard one-size-fits-all products, the growth of the consumer movement will not let it happen. The days of large consumer segments buying standard products have gone. The new market reality places competitive importance on the ability to manage a diversity of product offerings. Traditional cost systems mask the impacts from both diversity and variety and are providing highly inaccurate data.

Figure 2-13 graphically describes the resulting difference between traditional product costing and ABC product costing. The dashed horizontal line shows zero percent deviation from traditionally calculated product, the baseline cost. The vertical axis is the percent error deviation between the traditional and new ABC calculation.

On the horizontal axis individual part or product numbers (or services) are ranked left-to-right, from the most overcosted to the most undercosted. Although the shift in total overhead costs among products exactly nets to zero, the shaded areas will not be equal because the percent deviation on the vertical axis does not reflect volume; it is on a per-unit basis.

Note how large the differences are. Errors are not 5% to 10%. They are 50% to more than 1,000%. Logarithmic-scaled graphs are needed to fit the measured error on a single page! This result has given rise to a popular observation: it is better to be approximately correct than precisely inaccurate.[2]

---

[2]*Relevance Lost: The Rise and Fall of Management Accounting*, by H. Thomas Johnson and Robert S. Kaplan, Boston, Harvard Business School Press, 1987.

Diversity, complexity, and product variety are satisfactorily handled in ABC/ABM. The design team strives to show diversity by examining the amount and extent of cost behavior that each activity contains. Cost behavior is linked to cost objects based on unique distinctions and features in the cost objects that consume each separate activity.

Generally, products on the left side of the graph have high unit volumes, large lot sizes, limited engineering and technical support, minimal technology, and low complexity. Products on the right side of the graph have low unit volumes, small lot sizes, considerable engineering and technical support, and a large technology investment.

The height of the horizontal S-curve represents the degree of diversity. The ABC S-curve correctly reveals the distortions caused by traditional cost system misallocations. It shows a dramatically more accurate cost of products or services.

Figure 2-13.
PERCENT OVER
AND UNDER
PRODUCT COST

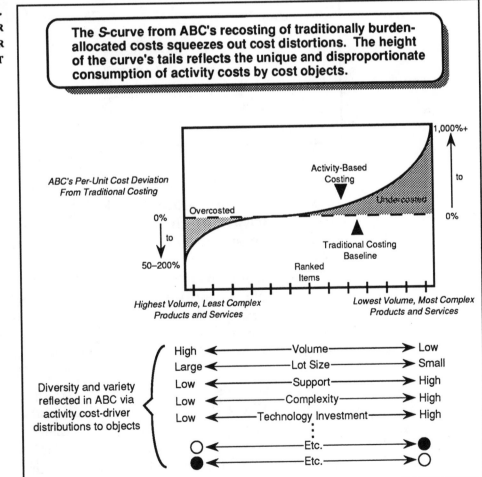

Seeing the Overall Picture

The shift in product costs illustrated by the S-curve in Figure 2-13 is only part of the big picture. An alarming view of ABC-computed profit is revealed when the ABC costs are matched with the total volume and sales dollars for *each* product or service sold.

Figure 2-14.
PRODUCT PROFIT-
ABILITY PROFILE

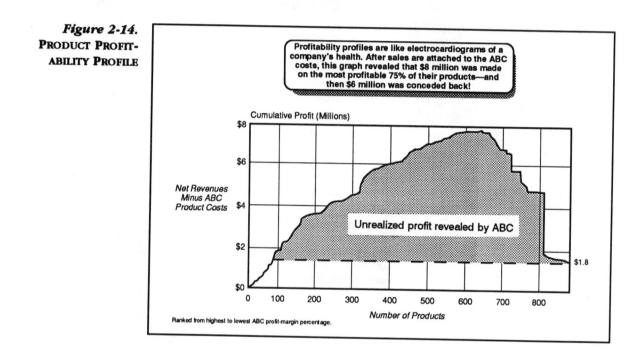

> Profitability profiles are like electrocardiograms of a company's health. After sales are attached to the ABC costs, this graph revealed that $8 million was made on the most profitable 75% of their products—and then $6 million was conceded back!

Cumulative Profit (Millions)

Net Revenues Minus ABC Product Costs

Unrealized profit revealed by ABC

$1.8

Number of Products

Ranked from highest to lowest ABC profit-margin percentage.

Figure 2-14 shows cumulative ABC dollar profit, by product, based on highest-to-lowest ranked product margins. The **$1.8** million profit at the right is correct and auditable; the steep incline and descent are, in effect, unrealized profits and losses simply displayed by ABC.

The conclusion is that companies have the potential to make a greater profit on individual items than managers ever imagined. However, this profit also can be lost simultaneously. Financial profit and loss statements report only the correct *total* profit. ABC reveals how products contribute to that profit (or loss), product by product.

Management's initial reaction to the right side of the graph shown in Figure 2-14 is to consider dropping unprofitable products. Some semifixed costs such as the maintenance or inspection functions may remain, however. These semifixed costs may cause an overhead death spiral when applied to the surviving products' costs because the unprofitable products may go away but not all of the costs. Additional analysis of each data point leads managers to consider other options, such as:

- Repricing,
- Rationalizing product variety (consolidation and elimination),
- Changing minimum order policies,
- Purchasing some loss products from a clueless competitor and repackaging them for resale,
- Increasing product sales volume,
- Redesigning the product or service (for example, design for manufacturability),
- Eliminating low value-added activities to reduce cost,
- Improving activity efficiency and reengineering processes,
- Reexamining site strategies,
- Reconsidering outsourcing,
- Accepting the situation with understanding of the impact (do nothing).

Regardless of management's reaction, having a product profitability profile is better than acting blindly without one. Management's response to this profile is, at least, an informed response. Companies with a product profitability profile have a competitive advantage.

Parts and products do not cause all overhead and activities. Customers, markets, and channels of distribution also cause costs. Suppliers acknowledge that the same manufactured product can cost significantly more to sell to one customer than to another. Section 7 explains how the ABC framework also can measure customer costs and their profitability, from the supplier's viewpoint. The ABC model simply adds customers as cost objects. The calculation method for products and customers is identical and effectively seamless.

A Word of Caution for ABC Users

ABC is not a silver bullet. Here is a caveat—using ABC for costing cost objects such as products does have shortcomings. ABC reports a cost/time slice with full period expensing and no consideration to amortizing long-term payback expenses, except those formally accounted for, such as depreciation. For example, in research and development, a large amount of expense for an abbreviated time period will be traced to a product, thus overinflating the product's cost. Similar distortions can occur for seasonal products. All products have a life cycle with front-end loading, involving prototypes and testing. Eventually, they need less care and attention, and costs stabilize. ABC measures cost consumption only for the period duration. Life-cycle product costing, though not popular today, likely will be launched from insights gained via ABC.

In addition, target costing and simultaneous engineering, which occur at the front end of this life cycle, are substantially enhanced with ABC data. Design engineers are furnished with quantified downstream costs that currently are hidden from them and are nonvalue adding.

ABC is regularly called a model as opposed to a system, because it is an "as-is" snapshot of the current state and conditions. ABM allows us to use these data for gain. Predictive modeling with activity-based data and relationships can generate proposed "to-be" pictures of future costs.

Now that we understand the cost-assignment model behind ABC, in Section 3 we can learn the more critical lessons involving the managing of costs using the same principles of cost consumption via drivers.

3. Activity-Based Management

ABC/ABM's Dual Axes

Activity-based accounting serves as both an accurate product-costing tool and a performance-improvement tool. Examine Figure 3-1. The cost-assignment view on the vertical axis (ABC) assigns resource

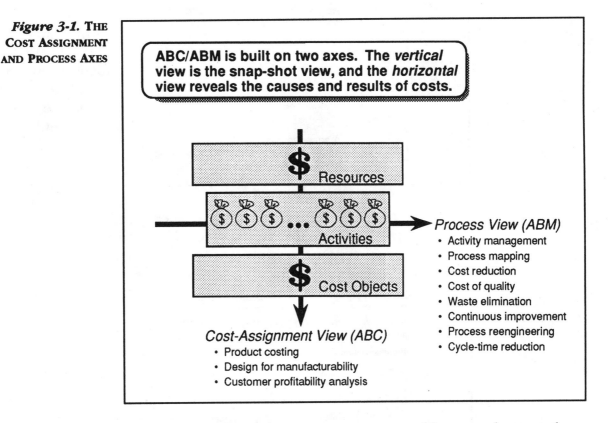

Figure 3-1. THE COST ASSIGNMENT AND PROCESS AXES

ABC/ABM is built on two axes. The *vertical* view is the snap-shot view, and the *horizontal* view reveals the causes and results of costs.

$ Resources

$ Activities

$ Cost Objects

Process View (ABM)
- Activity management
- Process mapping
- Cost reduction
- Cost of quality
- Waste elimination
- Continuous improvement
- Process reengineering
- Cycle-time reduction

Cost-Assignment View (ABC)
- Product costing
- Design for manufacturability
- Customer profitability analysis

costs to activities and activity costs to cost objects, such as products and customers. The process view on the horizontal axis (ABM) concentrates on managing processes and their constituent activities plus evaluating activity performance. ABM provides activity-based information to focus employee efforts on continuously improving quality, time, service, cost, flexibility, and profitability.

✦ ✦ ✦ ✦ ✦

Concentrating on the cost-assignment view increases product cost accuracy. This accuracy in turn leads to better strategic decisions for pricing, product mix, sourcing, and product design. The process view provides an operational and tactical tool to improve performance.

✦ ✦ ✦ ✦ ✦

Figure 3-2.
COST-ASSIGNMENT
VIEW

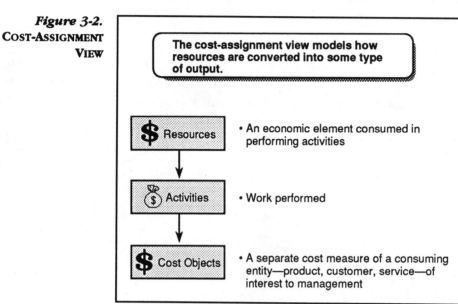

Regardless of activity accounting's use for product costing or process management, the best use for ABC/ABM is to help managers manage. ABC/ABM focuses on priorities and drives employee behavior, shifting toward an increased mix of products and markets. Figure 3-2 shows how resources are converted into output, as explained previously.

Figure 3-3 shows that an operational cost driver causes activities to use resources for accomplishing work and yielding output. These kinds of data are used for diagnostics and deeper analysis.

Figure 3-3.
THE PROCESS
VIEW

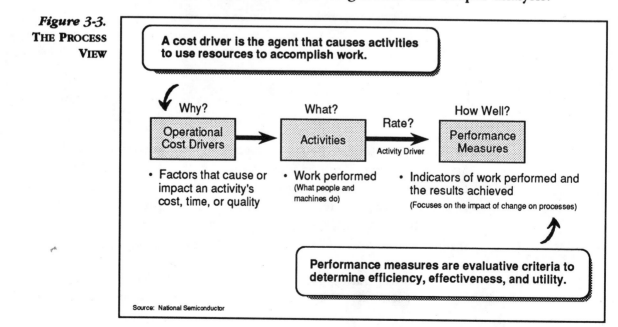

Source: National Semiconductor

Defining Activities and Their Level of Detail

The capability both to value products, services, and customer costs using ABC and to analyze activities and processes using ABM introduces a problem, caused by the increased flexibility of using activities as a fundamental building block. The problem is that this dual capability may confuse ABM system designers when they attempt to specify an activity's level of detail.

Detailed definitions of activities are not absolutely necessary to improve product cost accuracy. The key is in defining activities that can be summarized broadly. As described in Section 2, using appropriate activity drivers, mainly nonunit-volume drivers, corrects most of the misallocations caused by spreading overhead costs based only on labor or machine hours. Cross subsidies of under- or overcosted products are corrected sufficiently by a limited number of activity and activity-driver definitions. Extensive detail is not worthwhile for improving the accuracy of product or customer costing because of diminishing returns from incremental expansion and subdivision of activities. The amount of detail should be no greater than required by the purpose for which the data are to be used (see Figure 3-4).

More detailed information is necessary, however, on activities

Figure 3-4.
**DEFINING
ACTIVITY DETAIL**

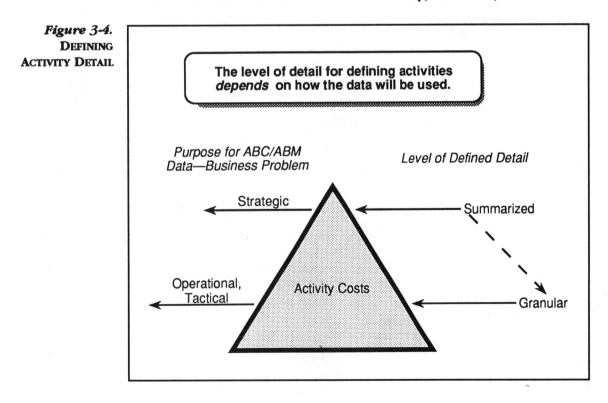

that benefit operational managers and assist them in influencing activities at a tactical level. At the tactical level, the trade-off is added detail versus the added cost to collect more data.

The most difficult part of ABC model designing is to define activities at an appropriate level of detail to satisfy the primary and predetermined purpose for the system. ABC designs for strategic purposes, such as product-mix profitability, use high-level summarized activities and are updated infrequently. Designs for operational purposes, such as cost reduction, use a low level of detail and refinement of activities and are updated more frequently.

❖ ❖ ❖ ❖ ❖

Do not mistake initial ABC pilots as a replacement for the financial accounting system that serves investors and regulators. ABC is a managerial system, and the interval between updates depends on user requirements and the rapidity of change (for example, new equipment, new products, changed processes, different employee jobs, and so forth). Eventually, ABC will interface directly with the general ledger, but today this interfacing would distract from a project team's objective—to have managers and employees accept ABC/ABM.

❖ ❖ ❖ ❖ ❖

Next we discuss the roles of activities and drivers and put them in the context of managing or altering processes for improvement.

The Role of Activities

Activities are central and critical to an ABM system. If they are well defined initially, the implementation project will overcome any problems. Businesses are asking questions that can help determine the level of detail and intentions required to define activities. Business and operations managers rarely begin by asking:

- How much am I spending to move materials?
- How much am I spending to order parts?
- How much am I spending to fix breakdowns?

Instead, managers are asking:

- What is the cost of complexity?
- What is the cost of waste in the system?
- How much is a ten percent improvement in reliability worth?
- What is the cost of idle capacity and where is it?
- How do I increase throughput?
- What should I focus on?
- What should be changed?

The answer to these questions lies in knowing the cost and value-added content of activities within processes and how costs change with changes in the mix of activities and redesign of processes. Therefore, the initial ABC/ABM model design should begin with questions that a business is asking to solve its problems. Activities must be defined so that these questions are answered. If the definition and assignment of dollars to activities are poorly planned in pilot models, the entire model will be viewed as useless by its users and probably will delay future upgrades to the enhanced and advanced cost management system.

There are many correct model designs, so it is advantageous to focus the design on a specific objective or problem set. Focusing the model design emphasizes certain activities by using key words or phrases to define an activity or by directing an activity definition toward influencing certain behavior. For example, if a company has a total quality management (TQM) campaign, the model should emphasize quality through waste elimination and conformance to expectations. If a company is pursuing a customer satisfaction, cycle time reduction, or time-to-market campaign, the model should be flavored accordingly with relevant campaign phrases. For a model to succeed, it must incorporate the values that management endorses.

An ABC/ABM project is more likely to succeed if the project team understands the problems of potential users. The team should try to find out in advance how users will use these new cost data.

The Role of Activity and Operational Cost Drivers

An activity driver measures how much of an activity is used by a cost object. It is a measure of output and is integral to ABC product costing. An activity driver provides a bridge linking ABC's informational elements—a bridge that distributes activity dollars into cost objects. However, if the activity driver does not redistribute activity dollars into each cost object in some proportion to some diversity unique to that cost object, the design team has missed the objective and continues to introduce error into product and cost object data.

Activity drivers may not be the true drivers of cost in the sense of triggering or being the root cause of an activity. The true drivers are called operational cost drivers. Activity drivers are consequences of what has happened, whereas operational cost drivers reveal what is making it happen. Costs tend to be incurred at the process level, not at the activity level. Operational cost drivers are factors that influence a change in cost of several related activities, whereas activity cost drivers measure the frequency and intensity of the demands placed on activities by output-oriented cost objects.

Because activity drivers are integral to product (or cost object) costing, they must be measurable, for example, the number of setups or material moves. In contrast, operational cost drivers may be less measurable but more insightful or directional as a cause, such as inventory levels or machine schedule imbalances. Operational cost measures are more useful for measuring performance because they are highlighted at a causal point, but the activity driver is usually easier to use for measuring performance as an output.

Activity drivers and the operational cost driver's work units for performance measures use similar data that may have different purposes. An activity driver mirrors the *consumption* of an activity by its cost objects. The operational cost driver mirrors *how efficiently* an activity (or group of activities) is performed (see Figure 3-5).

Figure 3-5.
ACTIVITY DRIVERS ARE COSTED OUT

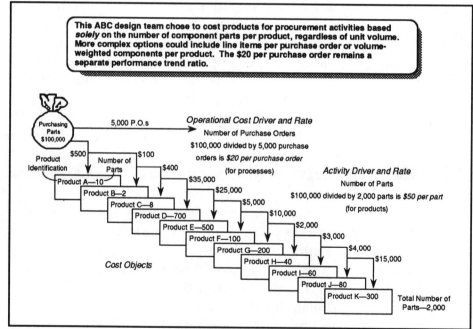

An activity driver for issuing purchase orders could be the number of parts on the product's bill of materials. This consumption measure does not reveal the efficiency of this activity. The output of issuing purchase orders is the operational cost driver—the number of purchase orders issued. A performance measure for issuing purchase orders could be the cost of each purchase order issued.

In Section 4, we discuss how additional managerial information can be attached to each activity in the form of attributes.

4. The Third Dimension— The Power of Attributes

Benchmarking, business process reengineering, and performance measurement are important to managers. ABC/ABM can facilitate an increasingly fair computation of measures that aid comparisons, such as plant-to-plant, without the apples-to-oranges problems that managers currently confront.

Before we address these subjects, this section describes how activity-based data can include additional managerial information, such as quality or time-speed, in the form of attributes. *These more comprehensive activity-based data then become a truly powerful tool not only for strategic and tactical use but also for behavioral change management.*

How Attributes Turn Hunches into Facts

Attributes are descriptive labels given to activities. A popular attribute is one for nonvalue-added activities. Attributes make activities robust. As shown in Figure 4-1, they are the third dimen-

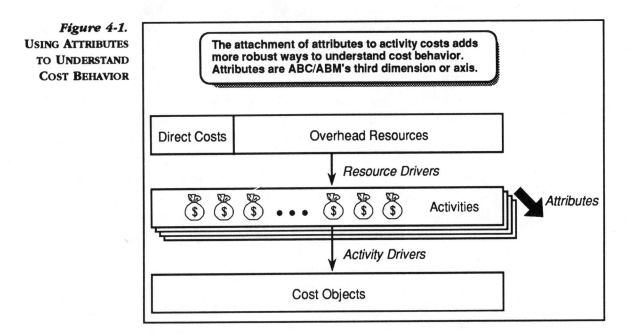

Figure 4-1.
USING ATTRIBUTES
TO UNDERSTAND
COST BEHAVIOR

The attachment of attributes to activity costs adds more robust ways to understand cost behavior. Attributes are ABC/ABM's third dimension or axis.

Direct Costs | Overhead Resources

Resource Drivers

$ $ $ ... $ $ $ Activities Attributes

Activity Drivers

Cost Objects

sion of the ABC model. Activity attributes are an orderly way to accumulate data for business decisions. Attributes quantify different aspects of business processes, and they provide multiple concurrent views with which to focus, prioritize, analyze, and measure.

Often companies intent on computing more accurate product costs using ABC pause after the first stage of collecting activity data. They begin using these fresh and valuable cost data to change processes before continuing with the next stage, costing products.

Activity analysis promotes creative ways to associate activities with attributes. Commonly used attributes include value-added content and cost-of-quality attributes. The types of attributes that companies may invent are unlimited. By using attributes, ABC supports emerging management improvement programs such as business process reengineering and benchmarking. ABC also supports related value-engineering and process-focused programs. Much is being said and written about shifting paradigms. The cost management discipline is changing to fit in with the new thinking on achieving customer satisfaction. It is effecting continuous improvement, as well as innovative breakthrough change for improvement.

Traditional cost management systems were intended to control costs using cost-based budgets, standards, variances, and narrowly reported measures for each responsibility cost center. The shift away from this budgeted cost variance paradigm has occurred for several reasons. First, financial accounting data for control purposes have been superseded by TQM-based quick-feedback systems, such as statistical process control. Second, as businesses downsize and become more cross-functional for increased flexibility and customer satisfaction, the focus is moving toward managing processes, many of which involve several different departments.

A business process is a string of sequential and related activities intended to achieve a specific goal. Costs may be measured as activities but incurred at the process level. Examples of common core business processes are purchasing items or enacting engineering changes. The new cost management paradigm focuses on understanding processes. Activity-based cost management data are deployed for prospective forward-planning diagnostic and analytical uses more than for control-intended after-the-fact scorekeeping.

ABC/ABM as a Change Management Tool

ABC/ABM should be thought of as a change-management tool. It is critical to understand processes. Once processes are understood, companies can achieve customer satisfaction, total quality management, time-based competition, and all the other popular strategies, campaigns, and programs used to initiate change within the enterprise.

Managers require answers to many questions so that they can understand their business environment. Attribute analysis is a way to answer the following and other questions:

- Why are there so many nonvalue-added costs?
- Why do costs of nonconformance exceed costs of conformance?
- What portion of costs actually can be controlled locally with responsibility?
- What portion of overhead costs vary with unit-volume or with batches or are specifically product-sustaining, technology-sustaining, or customer-sustaining costs?

The success of installing an ABC/ABM model depends greatly on the level of acceptance by its potential users. Do not expect users and employees to feel comfortable immediately with ABM. Initially, ABM may be viewed as an accounting gimmick, but attributes gain user attention. The insights that managers gain by using attributes tend to create interest for continuously using and refining the ABM model.

Figure 4-2 gives activities a three-dimensional appearance when attributes are added to each individual activity. Building ABC/ABM

Figure 4-2.
ACTIVITY ATTRIBUTES

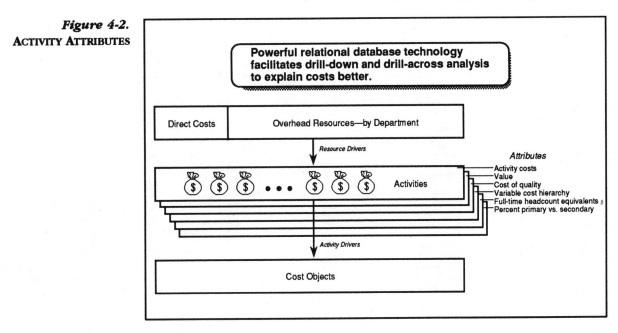

models and systems has been made easier using commercially available ABC software.

Various ABC-pioneering companies have imaginatively defined different types of attributes. Because of team creativity, new types of attributes probably will continue to appear.

Attributes are attached to activity costs. The initial use for activity costs is to rank activities by dollar amount and show them to employees and managers. People either are shocked at how they really spend money or they have their expectations confirmed. Either way, activity data provide useful feedback. Someday, ABC may be nicknamed "amnesty-based costing"—it brings out so much more of the costs that previously were masked by misallocation practices, but management should declare an amnesty and not use this information as a club. It is for purposes of understanding what people and machines do.

Examples of Popular Attributes

Value-Added Versus Nonvalue-Added Costs

This classification technique (see Figure 4-3) is popular because it allows the prioritizing of eventual action steps important for gaining ABC/ABM acceptance. Assigning grades on a scale is straightforward, but defining rules to assign these grades can be a challenge. Many companies define key value-added activities from a customer's

Figure 4-3.
VALUE-ADDED VS.
NONVALUE-
ADDED COSTS

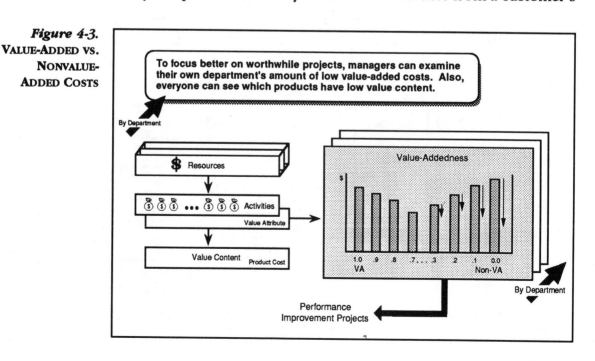

viewpoint. One asks, "Given a choice, would a customer pay for this activity?" or "If you quit performing this activity, will the customer notice or care?"

An external customer's viewpoint usually is used to define the scale for value-added content, but an internal customer's viewpoint also can work in a complex enterprise. Some activities are mandated by government legislation, such as from the Food and Drug Administration; they may be coded outside the value-added scale.

Business Process Reengineering

Processes such as administering engineering change orders can be evaluated by combining two or more activities that have a common purpose. Figure 4-4 shows how collections of activities can

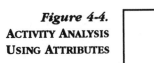

Figure 4-4.
ACTIVITY ANALYSIS
USING ATTRIBUTES

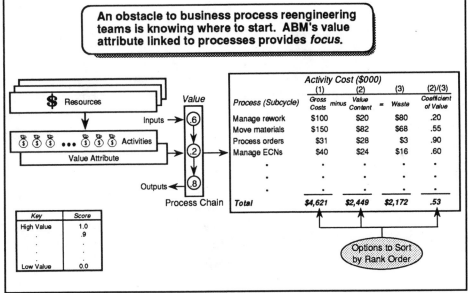

be ranked by gross dollar cost. By including the value-added attribute, processes can be compared and evaluated in terms of their size as well as value content.

Process value analysis using ABM data provides managers with a framework and a systematic approach for planning, predicting, and influencing cost. This approach focuses management attention on the interdependency between departments and functional activities. Also, by analyzing the cost drivers of activities within business processes, managers can understand and act on the causes of cost, not their symptoms.

Figure 4-5.
BUSINESS PROCESS
REENGINEERING

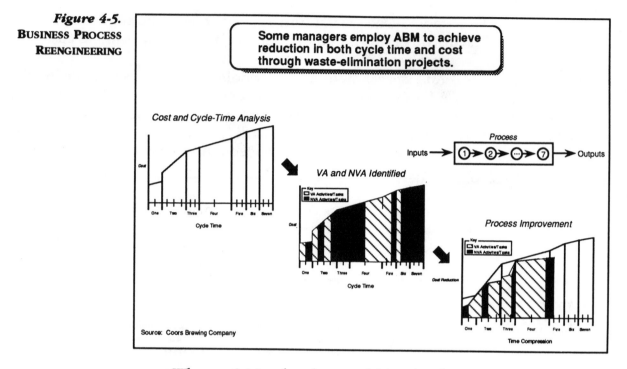

When activities that do not add much value are reduced or eliminated, both cost and time are improved, as shown in Figure 4-5. In Section 5, we will describe in more depth how ABM activity and attribute data are used to reengineer business processes.

Cost of Quality

This classification technique is consistent with the ideas of popular TQM leaders such as Crosby, Juran, and Deming. As shown in Figure 4-6, this technique places overhead activities into the following categories:

- Cost of conformance:
  - ▼ Prevention activities,
  - ▼ Appraisal activities;
- Cost of nonconformance:
  - ▼ Internal defect or failure activities,
  - ▼ External defect or failure activities.

Direct labor costs are necessary to convert materials and add value. Because these labor activities are direct costs, they may be excluded from the overhead cost-of-quality categories mentioned above. Some companies estimate that their costs of conformance and nonconformance exceed 80% of their overhead costs. These costs can be reduced by employing TQM techniques such as root-cause analysis or employing process-value analysis. Reducing the cost of nonconformance is important, but cost of conformance activities also should be considered as a target for improvement. All TQM activities have a cost that can be reduced.

❖ ❖ ❖ ❖ ❖

Some companies are disappointed by the lack of actions following their TQM training programs. They claim difficulty in getting started. ABC/ABM cost-of-quality data, which are relatively easy to score, provide a spark to jump start a quality program that has lost direction. Cost-of-quality metrics are controversial in TQM mainly because, in the past, users uncontrollably reclassified costs, sometimes including or excluding different cost types at each measure point.

ABC/ABM introduces a closed system wherein changes must occur either inside activities or as changes in activity-driver rates. ABC/ABM also substantiates any final cost-of-quality report with a list of detailed activities. In the past, computing a cost-of-quality number usually was done to satisfy an executive request, not to provide employees with a yardstick.

❖ ❖ ❖ ❖ ❖

In summary, activity attributes add more to activity analysis than just the costs of activities. Attributes make activities more understandable, usable, and meaningful. Attributes also provide leverage for decision making.

Figure 4-6.
COST OF
QUALITY

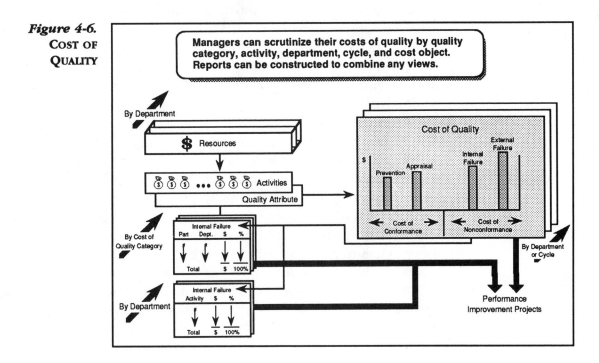

ABC/ABM is fundamentally a database measuring the current conditions and rates of resource cost consumption. ABC/ABM's potential is unleashed when users manipulate the data by sorting and reorganizing activity costs, activity cost drivers, and outputs to create different reports with various attributes.

If the project team does not make changes or make decisions any differently with the new data, the team's implementation basically has failed—it becomes a nonevent. The use of ABC/ABM data to make changes should be considered as a test of the success of the implementation. Next, we discuss some tips to consider that depend on whether the goal is ABC or ABM.

Designing for Activity-Based Product Cost and Activity-Based Management

An activity-based product cost model, or macro model, is generally less complex than other options. This model is also typical of early, first-generation ABC efforts. In the past, the users of the new data were usually financially oriented. Product decisions from the ABC data usually involve product pruning and rationalizing and optimizing the product mix. The design team will define activities in general terms and sensibly limit the number and diversity of activities. The outcome of the model is significantly improved product costs. The model will require updating as business conditions change, perhaps annually. Changes that lead to different activities or swings in the size of activities require updating the model. Such changes include introducing new products, abandoning old products, or introducing new equipment, technology, skilled positions, or services.

Activities are used to capture and interpret data. When constructing a macro model, the level of detail for defining activities should not be more refined than the level of insight needed for decision making. The challenge is to keep this balance during design. The temptation to overdesign is strong, and ABC software does not act as a deterrent. An activity-based management model, or micro model, is generally more complex and refined than the macro model. Figure 4-7 shows the contrast between macro and micro model design. Note how the micro activity data are captured at the lower levels of an indented bill of activities. It is this ability to roll up and consolidate micro activities into macro activities for product costing (ABC) that allows multiple uses of activity data in the same ABC/ABM system.

Figure 4-7.
MACRO VS.
MICRO DESIGN

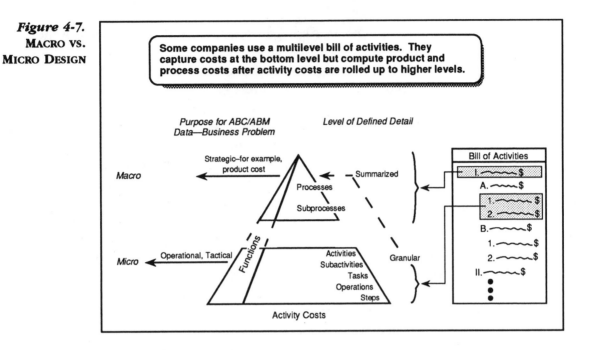

Some companies use a multilevel bill of activities. They capture costs at the bottom level but compute product and process costs after activity costs are rolled up to higher levels.

Sequencing of the ABC/ABM system design can be approached in two ways. Some companies focus first on product cost (ABC) and then on performance management (ABM). Other companies focus first on performance management (ABM) and then on product cost. For companies that focus on continuous improvement using ABM, the primary goal is process improvement.

✢ ✢ ✢ ✢ ✢

As an example, National Semiconductor Corporation, an advanced user, recognized that the two views—cost-assignment (ABC) and process view (ABM)—serve two different management groups. The design team took advantage of this knowledge by defining micro activities to meet the needs of the managers who are directly responsible for performance. Defining micro activities allowed a manager to begin process improvements immediately. The micro activities later were consolidated into relevant product costing-oriented macro activities. The ABC/ABM team addressed both management groups without creating the massive amount of data of two models or sacrificing the needs of one group for the needs of the other.

✢ ✢ ✢ ✢ ✢

Management efforts for TQM or total cycle time reduction may yield results initially but frequently are not effective in the long run because of a lack of reliable activity cost information. TQM projects suffer from an absence of financial metrics. ABM provides these useful metrics. The micro model addresses business issues more than product cost. The users of the ABM model include engineering and operations management, whose goal, to improve the process, is constant.

Some design rules for combining micro activities into macro activities using an indented bill of activities are as follows:

- Activities should have the same level of variability. For example, a batch-level activity should not be combined with a unit-level activity. A product-sustaining activity should not be combined with a batch-level activity. A facility-sustaining activity should not be combined with other nonfacility-sustaining activities.
- Activities with similar variability should be assigned the same activity driver. This assignment ensures that the activity driver used for each macro activity reflects the activity consumption in a level, linear, and nondistorting manner.
- Activities should be similar in function, to ensure that activities requiring separate visibility receive it even if they use the same activity driver.

In summary, if companies understand the two views used to design the ABC/ABM system before beginning a project, they can capture activity data initially at a sufficient level of detail to serve tactical and operational purposes. For strategic purposes, individual activities can be combined and rolled up into summary, or macro, activities, which are attached to products using a single activity driver. Individual activities also can be combined and rolled up into different macro activities (than those used for product costing), which equate to processes.

Section 5 discusses the emerging subjects of benchmarking and business process reengineering.

5. ABM Benchmarking and Business Process Redesign and Reengineering

Benchmarking is a 1990s form of copying from the masters, similar to what apprentices do. Benchmarking involves sharing and full disclosure between partners. By predefining and standardizing in advance both activity and activity driver definitions, multiple sites can compare themselves on a level playing field.

Figure 5-1.
ABC BENCH-
MARKING

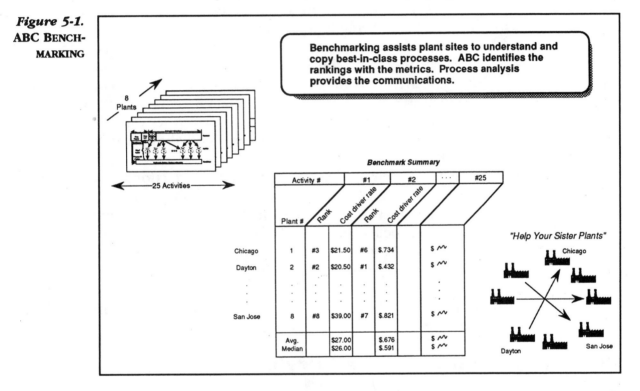

Benchmarking assists plant sites to understand and copy best-in-class processes. ABC identifies the rankings with the metrics. Process analysis provides the communications.

Figure 5-1 shows how eight internal plant sites are able to rank themselves from worst to best for individual processes, using ABM data. The activity driver per unit of process output is the measuring rod. Substandard performers now have data to analyze what better practices are required to be the best. More important, they have partners who will disclose how their best-in-class process achieves superior measurable results.

Although a process comprises multiple activities, for bench-

41

marking, consider a process as synonymous with an activity.

Why is business process redesign and reengineering becoming a popular management campaign? First, leading-edge companies coined the phrase "bleeding edge" when they observed their competitors rapidly copy their products without incurring the expenses of research and development. The lesson learned is that superior business and manufacturing processes offer greater and more sustainable advantages than products. Superior processes provide long-term advantages and are more difficult for competitors to copy.

Second, it is no longer sufficient to endorse continuous productivity improvement as an incremental and gradual journey. Outright breakthrough innovation must be combined with continuous improvement. Companies first must do the right things, and then do the right things well. Business process redesign and reengineering encourages this behavior; its war cry, coined by the productivity consultant Michael Hammer, is "don't automate, obliterate!" In effect, companies are realizing they cannot afford their existing overhead and infrastructure, and they have to act more quickly.

Finally, downsizing and work force reductions, together with mission-critical cross-functional coordination, are resulting in a different employee base. Businesses are retaining more flexible workers to focus on and leverage the enterprise's core competencies, regardless of organizational structure and pecking order. Beyond some level of employee cutbacks, lean and stretched organizations can no longer simply remove bodies to improve profits. Instead, they must extract waste out of the system's business processes.

The Effect of Business Process Reengineering

Business process reengineering dramatically affects cost, quality, service, and speed. It is distinguished by results that are quantum leaps and order-of-magnitude improvements, rather than just the day-to-day continuous improvements preached by quality management devotees. To accomplish innovation and breakthrough changes requires creative, step-out-of-your-box thinking and solutions. It further requires the cross-functional redesign of major processes. This redesign becomes an expansion of scope for stovepipe managers who are limited to office talk about what is upstream and downstream from them but who now must get involved. Business process reengineering is certainly not business as usual.

Figure 5-2.
ABM AND
BUSINESS
PROCESS
REENGINEERING

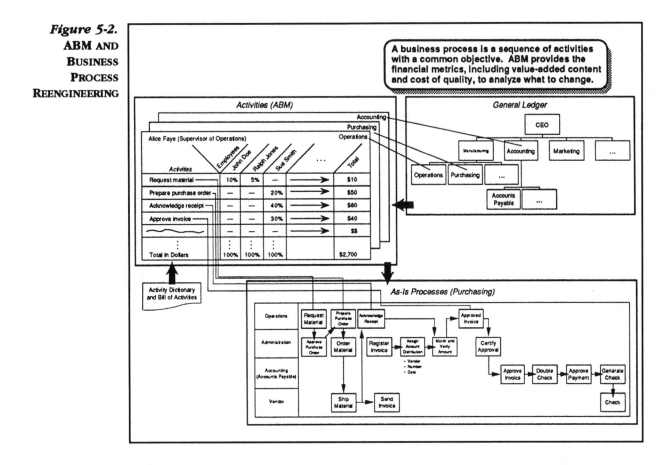

Figure 5-2 shows how ABM data are linked to processes. A business process is a sequence of two or more activities with a common purpose. Costs are incurred at the process level and are measurable at the activity level. The link of activity costs and their attributes (for example, value-added content, cost of quality, and so forth) with time-sequenced process steps provides the power for new insights.

At the bottom of Figure 5-2, a traditional flow chart reveals how items are worked on and passed across work stations such as departments or functions. Note that the resource drivers from the input form exactly equate to the activities in the flow chart. This is not an accident. With advanced planning, activity costs with their attributes can be mapped to "as-is" processes.

The next step is to develop and achieve a "to-be" process that will serve the customers of the process better—as well as faster and cheaper. ABC/ABM data join time-based and quality-based metrics for the brainstorming needed to make the migration from the "as-is" to the "to-be" happen.

Section 6 covers fresh uses of ABC/ABM data to gauge the consequences of changes in activities.

6. Understanding Cost Variability for Accurate Cost Estimating and Budgeting

On page 47 (Activity-Based Budgeting) we will find out how the "as-is" ABC/ABM model of cost consumption, including all its cost pools, rates, and parameters, is used to model outcomes predictively to solve problems. First, however, we deal with the thorny problems that are involved with truly fixed costs (the facility-sustaining costs listed in Figure 2-12).

The Myths of Full-Absorption Costing

Variable cost behavior analysis shows how the magnitude of activities varies with volume and mix changes of cost objects. Classifying activities means they can be matched systematically to activity drivers with similar variable behavior. This analysis is critical for simulating "what if" scenarios that gauge the impact on cost of proposed changes in sales and production. This basic analysis is used for justifying investments, for cost estimating new business and orders, and for cost budgeting.

As discussed in Section 2, ABC provides greater insight into the behavior of costs than traditional fixed-versus-variable cost analysis. There are facility-sustaining costs such as recruiting, janitorial services, security officers, and rent and insurance. These costs are depicted as nontraceable overhead to the right in Figure 6-1. Such costs are not caused by products or customers, which makes it difficult, if not impossible, to attach them to products or customers.

Facility-sustaining costs do not have direct cause-and-effect relationships with primary business functions and processes. ABC model designers are encouraged to minimize the size of facility-sustaining costs by aggressively examining the costs to see if they might be caused by any activity.

For example, fractions of the time spent by executive officers can be linked to some of the same activities their subordinates spend time on. Eventually, only costs with the highest fixed or extremely

Figure 6-1.
FACILITY-SUSTAIN-
ING COSTS

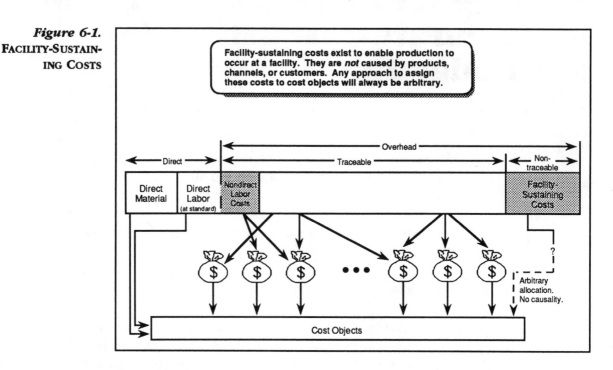

Figure 6-1.
FACILITY-SUSTAIN-
ING COSTS

discretionary content will remain as a residual—the truly facility-sustaining costs.

When companies perform traditional cost estimating to bid for orders or new business, they add a tax-like cost-plus surcharge to recover the so-called fixed costs. Companies using the substantially expanded cost elements from ABC data are learning to assign the recovery of these truly fixed costs selectively to specific products or customers. This distribution is not accomplished by spreading costs evenly based on sales dollars or any other assumed link. Rather, the disconnect between these costs and any cost object is first recognized. Then the costs are associated with those customers (or products) that can absorb them. The purpose for associating costs when there is no causality is for inclusion in quoting prices for new businesses.

Figure 6-2 displays how this practice gives the sales function a greater range for pricing, which may prove an advantage in bidding for an order or customer. The primary caution, however, is not to continue to price too many orders in this manner because the older base business eventually will expire without sufficient price coverage for the truly fixed costs.

❖ ❖ ❖ ❖ ❖

Companies eventually begin to understand that products do not cause facility-sustaining costs. Despite this understanding, a company may insist that products absorb all costs. This insistence occurs because companies like to analyze profit margins that show the recovery or absorption of all costs. If a company insists on absorption of all costs, it can spread facility-sustaining costs after all direct and activity-based costs have been traced to cost objects. A reasonable allocation base could be the cumulative ABC costs for total product cost, because, at that point, all products will have been costed based on logic—a cost profile not to be distorted.

❖ ❖ ❖ ❖ ❖

Activity-Based Budgeting or Activity-Requirement Planning (ARP)

What follows are powerful ways to use ABC/ABM data for predictive modeling. Activity-based budgeting is the reverse engineering of the ABC cost-assignment framework. By estimating the quantities and volumes over a future time period for all the cost objects and activity cost drivers, the level of resource costs can be computed. This technique is effectively an elaborate flexible budget; however, it uses more factors than simply estimated units of output or labor hours.

To readers who are familiar with the inventory production method called material requirements planning (MRP), the reverse explosion math for placing purchase orders is strikingly similar. ARP places demands on activities in a way that is very much like the way MRP places demands on suppliers. Activity costs are then translated

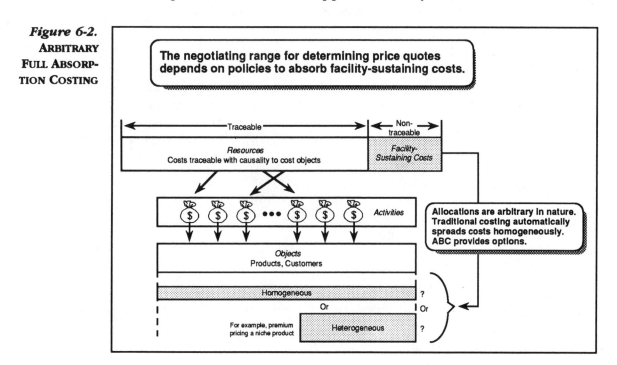

Figure 6-2.
ARBITRARY FULL ABSORPTION COSTING

The negotiating range for determining price quotes depends on policies to absorb facility-sustaining costs.

Traceable — Non-traceable

Resources
Costs traceable with causality to cost objects

Facility-Sustaining Costs

$ $ $ ••• $ $ $ *Activities*

Allocations are arbitrary in nature. Traditional costing automatically spreads costs homogeneously. ABC provides options.

Objects
Products, Customers

Homogeneous ?

Or Or

For example, premium pricing a niche product

Heterogeneous ?

into the mix and magnitude of resource costs. Refer to Figure 2-9 and imagine reverse-computing the ABC model. Assume the activity rates, calibrated from those that were used to construct the model initially.

This new predictive model is computing the amount of activities based on the estimated mix, quantities, and volumes of cost objects and activity drivers and also must equal the level of resources predictably consumed. Of course, this newly computed level of resources will never equal the enterprise's point-in-time payroll and indirect spending.

The difference is actually a computation of a capacity difference. ABC brings visibility to the areas that have excess (or deficient) capacity.

❖ ❖ ❖ ❖ ❖

Activity-based costing measures consumption, not spending. Changes in spending (for example, overtime, hiring, or downsizing) will always lag behind the changes in the mix and quantity of cost-object demand to which they are responding.

❖ ❖ ❖ ❖ ❖

Activity-based budgeting is appealing because it is consistent with the notion of continuous improvement. The estimated costs of resources can be computed immediately, as soon as estimates for cost objects and activity volumes are collected. The focus is on identifying and managing excess capacity. Activity-based budgeting also is appealing as a replacement for the traditional budget cycle because of criticisms of current budget practices. Criticisms include the following:

■ Employees expend a great amount of time and cost to produce the annual budget, with questionable benefits;

■ Data become stale in relation to rapid product changes, quick moves on the part of competitors, and continuous internal organizational changes during and after preparation of the budget;

■ The budget format is excessively organizational (for example, departmental), while simultaneously structure becomes less important and cross-functional integration becomes more relevant;

■ Spending control can be accomplished with alternatives, such as with signature approval policies;

■ After-the-fact budget variances usually reflect negotiating skills of supervisors at the beginning of the budget year and do not measure their performance reacting to the variables that realistically happen.

Activity-Based Cost Estimating for Quoting

The same logic behind activity-based budgeting and activity requirements planning currently is being used for quoting bids. Traditional quotes are constructed from rigorous estimates of the direct labor and material costs. Next, a spread percent factor is used, which presumes all new orders will consume overhead activities at an enterprise-wide average rate. This is nonsense.

An ABC cost estimate uses an activity-by-activity checklist. The quoted order is tested for its impact in placing demands on activities. For those activities impacted, the activity driver is multiplied by the quoter's estimate of driver volumes.

For example, will a 200,000-piece order require four setups of 50,000 units, or 20 setups of 10,000 units? The batch-related costs will differ.

Similar to the S-curve in product cost subsidizing, ABC logic accurately predicts how quoted orders will disproportionately place demands on all activities and processes. Then it costs them out, using its calibrated driver rates.

Controlling Acceptable Imprecision

In this section, we briefly discuss how ABC can tolerate some error without much adverse effect.

Design teams often consist of accountants and engineers, who have a tendency to create detailed models. ABC/ABM software does not deter teams from overengineering their models. Rather, it enables and encourages them to do so. These teams unknowingly can spend excessive time and energy to develop elaborate activity driver profiles that affect only a small fraction of total activity costs. Such detailed models may use activity costs with less-than-imaginative activity drivers.

In addition, design teams tend to define inappropriate activity drivers for cost objects, usually at too-detailed a level for the cost object. In this use, it is more acceptable to trace activities to a product brand or product family than to a specific product. It is also acceptable to trace activities to a market segment instead of to a particular customer. From this less-detailed level, cost can be spread by annual unit volume. At this point, the model has separated most of the significant cost diversity. This fact makes it acceptable to allocate, which we have been doggedly resisting. Developing the model from a less-detailed level minimizes distortion from misallocation. Figure 6-3 shows why acceptable levels of imprecision are okay.

Figure 6-3.
SIZING THE
ABC/ABM
SYSTEM

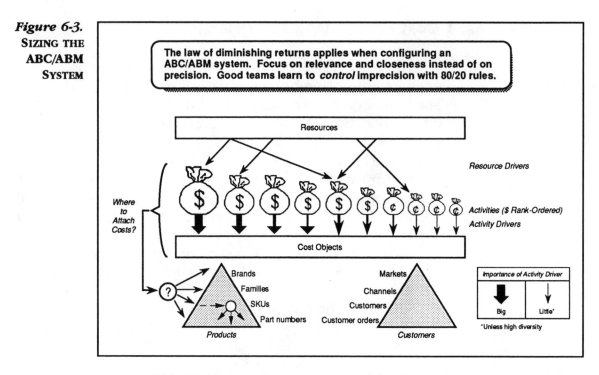

With ABC/ABM, closeness is much better and more practical than precision. Further, it is simpler, more economical, and produces fewer headaches.

In Section 7, we explore how nonmanufacturing activity costs, often white collar in nature, can be assigned directly to customers. Doing so facilitates understanding profitability by customer.

7. Understanding Customer Demands and Profitability

In Section 7, we explore how nonmanufacturing activity costs, which often are white-collar in nature, can be assigned directly to customers. This direct assignment facilitates understanding profitability by customer. Products do not cause all resource consumption, but they cause most manufacturing resource consumption. There are also many other types of resource consumption. Production planning, engineering, and sales offices are further removed from the manufacturing floor so that current production products have less impact on these types of white-collar resources.

Moving toward the sales office means that customers and channels of distribution have a greater impact on consumption of administrative resources. These customer and marketing costs of conducting business deserve the same attention as product costs.

As shown in Figure 7-1, a parallel cost continuum, in which the

Figure 7-1.
UNDERSTANDING
CUSTOMER
PROFITABILITY

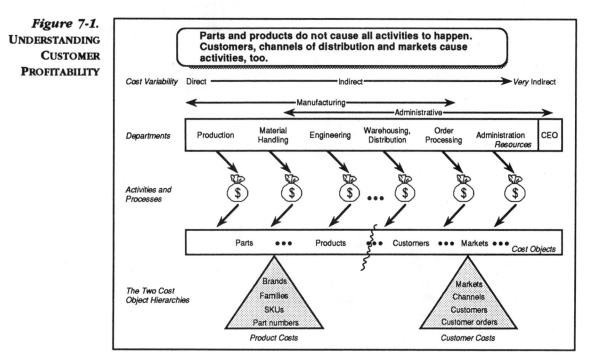

51

business function coincides with the associated cost objects, can be matched process by process. As this resource-cost continuum moves (left to right) from production to administrative functions, the cost-object continuum also moves from parts to customers and markets served.

❖ ❖ ❖ ❖ ❖

Note that the two main cost object families—products and customers—can be expressed in pyramidal hierarchies. This situation occurs because certain resources, such as a product engineer, cannot be attached at a part number level, but they can be charged higher in the hierarchy and then fanned or allocated to products within their product family.

❖ ❖ ❖ ❖ ❖

Figure 7-2.
CUSTOMER PROFIT-
ABILITY MATRIX

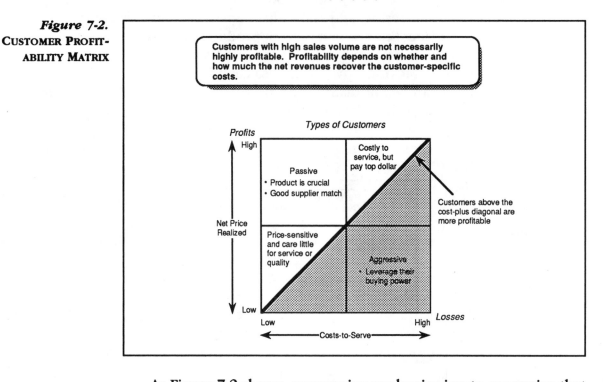

As Figure 7-2 shows, companies are beginning to recognize that customers with the highest sales volumes do not necessarily generate high profits. Figure 7-3 shows that the use of ABC principles provides companies with a more realistic view of the sources of profit. Sales and marketing costs consumed by specific customers or markets are combined with the ABC manufacturing stock-to-dock product costs to give this clearer view.

As consumer feature and function preferences become increasingly segmented without any relaxation of management edicts to maximize customer satisfaction, ABC will assist in making tough

Figure 7-3.
CUSTOMER
MIGRATION MATRIX

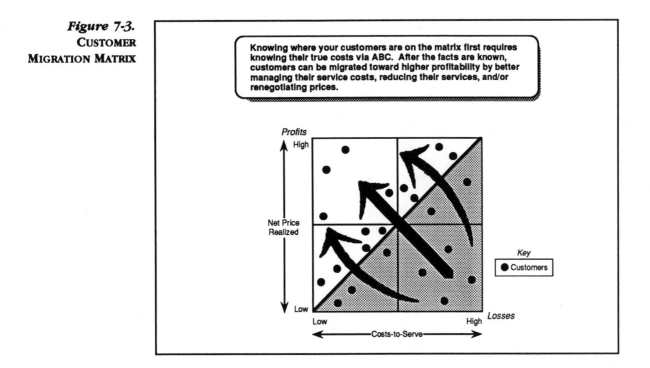

decisions. Consumer demands for affordable prices with prompt and reliable service will keep cost as a highly visible element of any evaluation equation, despite increasing attention to the elements of service, quality, and flexibility.

8. The Unification of Quality, Time, and Cost Data

Just as the falling of the Berlin Wall is today creating substantial changes throughout the globe, a similar monumental event is occurring in the business world. Organizations that have been forever vertically structured also are tearing something down. Businesses are recognizing that their stovepipe-like functional departments are impediments, and they are being tipped over to manage cross-functional processes better.

The popular business buzzword for this upset is business process redesign and reengineering. The jolt that has tipped over our organizational silos is the emergence of the idea that customer satisfaction is the only critical success factor; everything else is secondary. With this fresh thinking, manager-desired programs-of-the-month are giving way to customer-benefiting programs.

Although business process redesign or reengineering may sound like another this-too-shall-pass management program, this one is different because there is so much common sense involved. Check out this string of logic:

- A *process* is the integrating theme for the organization of work.
- A process consists of two or more *activities* having a common purpose, which usually involves a *customer* of some sort.
  - ▼ Activities are the foundation and building blocks for improvement programs.
    - *Total quality management* (TQM) is performing activities without error.
    - *Just-in-time* (JIT) flow control is doing activities without waste.
    - *Simultaneous engineering* is incorporating into design not only what customers want but also the features that will minimize the low-value-adding activities downstream, such as assembling, inspecting, reworking, or repairing.
  - ▼ In effect, *business process reengineering* synchronizes activities

across functional boundaries. It forces customer-desired, not department manager-desired, changes.

- A horizontal, cross-functional view of processes is essential because our current vertical organizational structure is notorious for repeatedly losing sight of the customer between department hand-offs.
  - ▼ Strong individuals and team heroics cannot compensate for poor processes.
  - ▼ When people collectively better understand their core processes and the purpose of those processes, they change things more quickly and radically.
  - ▼ The rate of organizational learning is a critical distinction between competitors, particularly in high-tech companies—which eventually is everybody.
- Investing in processes and process innovation offers sustainable advantages longer than products or services, which can always be copied by competitors.

Therefore, business process redesign and reengineering are the words for transforming our business processes to achieve radical breakthroughs more quickly and optimize the development of new products and their delivery to customers. Note how integral is the role of activities—what people and equipment do—to completing the string of logic above.

Unfortunately, business process redesign and reengineering involves both processes and organizational structure, as in who reports to whom. Both must change.

Business process reengineering is the radical redesigning of processes to speed the flow of materials, documents, communications, and decisions. Only by viewing processes side-by-side can one understand the obstacle course and hurdles that slow down the movements of the activities it takes to make customers happy. Companies finally can feel that they are making progress at accomplishing work faster, better, and cheaper—all three at once.

Quality programs focus on how to *improve* what people are doing. Reengineering, in contrast, focuses on *eliminating* what people are doing.

Business process reengineering is not blind head count reduction. It is not tinkering with incremental improvements. It is not cutting fat or just reorganizing people. It is not brute force automation to cement outdated procedures or simply to do the same archaic practices faster. What it does is realign resources with the customers they are intended to serve.

Agile Manufacturing

As the pace of change accelerates, tools and techniques are not leading the charge for performance improvement as much as is the integration of all the tools. ABC and JIT were in practice 50 years ago but under different names, such as material flow control. Today, all these managerial programs and philosophies have converged. Figure 8-1 presents a genealogy chart. It depicts agile manufacturing as the descendent of the many separately dedicated but currently merging advances in manufacturing.

Figure 8-1.
TOWARD AGILE
MANUFACTURING

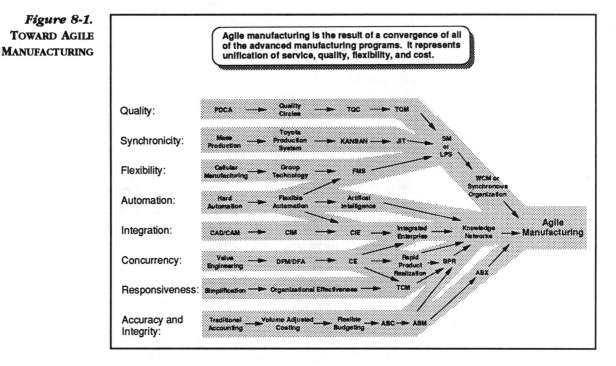

- *Quality*
  PDCA Plan, do, check, act
  TQC   Total quality control
  TQM   Total quality management
- *Synchronicity*
  JIT   Just-in-time
  SM   Synchronous manufacturing
  LPS   Lean production systems
- *Flexibility*
  FMS   Flexible manufacturing systems
  WCM   World-class manufacturing
- *Integration*
  CAD   Computer-aided design
  CAM   Computer-aided manufacturing
  CIM   Computer-integrated manufacturing
  CIE   Computer-integrated enterprise

- *Concurrency*
  DFM   Design for manufacturability
  DFA   Design for ease of assembly
  CE   Concurrent engineering
  BPR   Business process reengineering
- *Responsiveness*
  TCM   Total change management
- *Accuracy and Integrity*
  ABC   Activity-based costing
  ABM   Activity-based management
  ABX   Activity-based information

Agile manufacturing is the extreme polar opposite of Henry Ford's turn-of-the-century mass production route to riches. In the past, the consumer had no choice—exemplified by the black Model T—and volume-based economies of scale dominated decisions. Today, widely segmented consumer preferences are being courted under the banner of maximizing customer satisfaction. Agile manufacturing emphasizes flexibility so consumers can order one-of-a-kind products with quick delivery at affordable prices.

Historically, accounting's mission emphasized precision and control based on hindsight. Although activity-based costing and management (ABC/ABM) are introducing new and potentially powerful data for strategic use and for predictive planning by managers, accounting's reputation is tainted by its old fixation on numbers without relevance.

Most activity-based cost accounting systems are successful but when there is trouble, it often occurs when individuals are either uninformed of the system's purpose or have not experienced a system implementation. Because ABC/ABM projects compete with other initiatives such as total quality management (TQM), just-in-time (JIT), computer-integrated manufacturing (CIM), design for manufacturability (DFM), and so forth, managers may be reluctant to initiate such a project. To gain acceptance for advanced costing techniques based on activity-based measurements, managers must understand the following two principles:

- ABC/ABM does not necessarily require two sets of financial books for internal managerial and external regulatory purposes.
- It is imperative that managers realize how ABC/ABM fits together with other business improvement programs (such as TQM, DFM, and so forth), which use time-based and quality-based data (see Figure 8-2).

Misunderstandings about ABC occur because questions still remain from the first pilot ABC projects of the late 1980s. The debate revolves around the following two questions:

- Does activity-based accounting simply correct the distortions from the traditional allocation-based method and compute revised product costs with more accurate product profits?
- Or does ABC/ABM clarify the cost and degree of value added for activities and processes by restating general ledger-based reports into better information so managers can relate and respond regardless of what products cost?

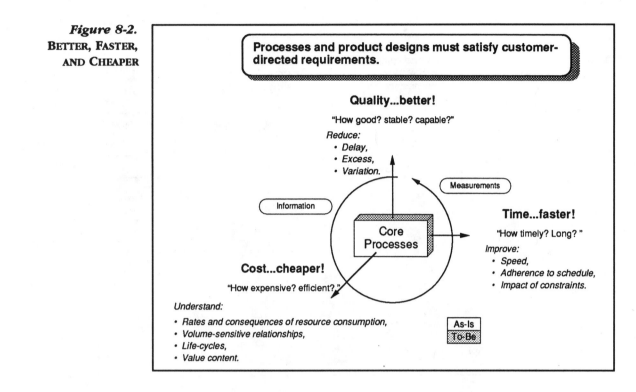

Figure 8-2.
BETTER, FASTER,
AND CHEAPER

The answers to these questions are that ABC/ABM accomplishes both these objectives, and more. Based on recent activity-based accounting projects in companies that use ABC software, a majority of project teams begin with a strong sense of the business problems that must be solved and then learn from trial and error. This discovery process is currently the best way to apply ABC/ABM and to use the ABC/ABM data.

Activity-Based Management Applications

Figure 8-3 catalogs the various activity-based management applications that ABC/ABM project teams pursue. When cost-based data are combined with quality-based and time-based data, results get even better. The extent of uses is broad because activity-based information acts as an enabler that empowers teams and task forces. The strength of this management tool is its ability to measure and organize data at an extremely fundamental level where resource-consuming activities are performed. ABC/ABM makes it easier to understand variable cost behavior information. It dramatically supersedes simplistic categorizing of costs as either fixed or variable with a superior continuous view of cost viscosity—within processes.

ABC/ABM also brings visibility to the degree of value-added cost

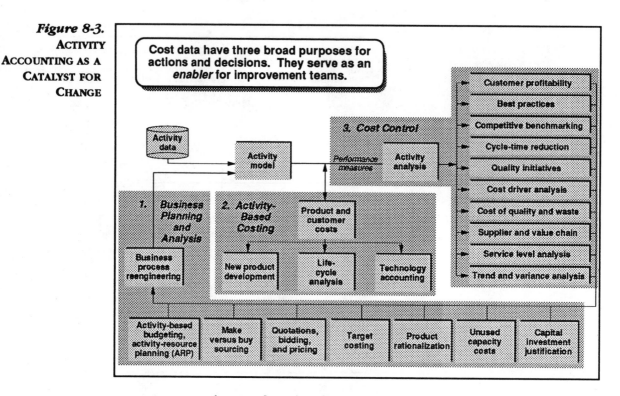

Figure 8-3.
ACTIVITY
ACCOUNTING AS A
CATALYST FOR
CHANGE

content and cost-of-quality for activities and processes. This information can be used to enhance continuous improvement and breakthrough innovation projects.

Natural laws describe how resources are consumed by activities. Four components of activity-based management systems have an impact on cost consumption:

- The *mix* of products, services, customers, and channels of distribution;
- The physical design features of and the specifications for *products*;
- The effects of *processes*, which often are influenced by formal or informal policies;
- The presence of *waste* due to neglect or errors of nonconformance.

These components cause costs to occur. As shown in Figure 8-4, insight gained from activity-based analysis will have a favorable impact on resource consumption by reducing or eliminating activities or by substituting a more economical alternative for an inefficient activity or unnecessary process. Today's popular corrective-action programs intended to control these components are product rationalization, design for manufacturability, and elimination of waste by reengineering processes.

ABC/ABM eventually will be adopted universally because traditional allocation-based costing methods actually misallocate and mask the causes of costs. With ABC/ABM, cost drivers link causes to cost consumption and remove this masking of cost behavior. Once product-cost distortions are corrected using activity-based tracing methods, management realizes that more profits are generated by fewer products than previously recognized. Managers also realize that offering too many unnecessary products and services substantially erodes profits. When managers understand the relationship between processes, products, and profits, they can take corrective action. They can abandon product lines, reprice, and target process improvements as candidates for reengineering.

Strategic applications for ABC/ABM are more obvious than tactical and operational applications. Controversy surrounds cost reporting as a control tool. For example, Eli Goldratt, a theory-of-constraints advocate, believes that cost accounting is the "number one enemy of productivity." Other professors, including H. Thomas Johnson of Portland State University, argue that cost control and reporting are not effective for improving process controls and efficiency. These controversies disappear as ABC information is used in conjunction with other improvement philosophies to focus improvement efforts profitably. The improved awareness that comes from the ABC/ABM process view will evolve with experience.

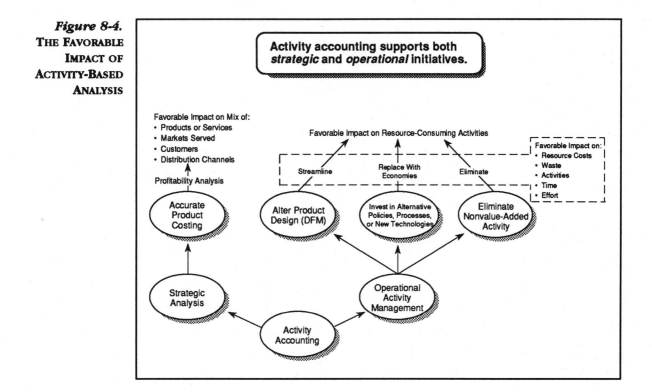

Figure 8-4.
THE FAVORABLE IMPACT OF ACTIVITY-BASED ANALYSIS

ABC/ABM will emerge much more as a planning and decision-making tool than as a method for after-the-fact reporting on control performance.

Companies can reduce difficulty getting started with ABC/ABM and TQM programs by initiating the discovery process using a repetitive plan-do-check-act (PDCA) approach. ABC/ABM systems should be designed at the same time that quality and process redesign teams construct root-cause diagrams, map processes, and so forth. All project teams eventually will unite and reconcile the different ways they define and account for activities within processes. ABC/ABM data serve initially as financial metrics to aid in identifying project opportunities (ABC's diagnostic phase) and, later, to stimulate ideas for options and alternative processes (ABC's analytical phase). After a team prioritizes and completes improvement projects, it uses ABC/ABM to measure the cost impact and consequences of change (measurement phase).

ABC's strategic value is its ability to correct product-cost distortion. ABM's operational value is in linking the fresh financial metrics of resource-cost consumption to improvement programs. Managers who understand ABC/ABM realize that accurate, relevant cost data enable them to identify and achieve innovation and continuous improvement.

References

Brimson, James. *Activity Accounting: An Activity-Based Costing Approach*. New York, John Wiley & Sons, 1991.

Brinker, Barry J. ed. *Emerging Practices in Cost Management* (a compilation of 50 articles from the *Journal of Cost Management*, Spring 1987 to Fall 1990). Boston, Warren, Gorham & Lamont, 1990.

Cooper, Robin, and Robert S. Kaplan. *The Design of Cost Management Systems: Text, Cases and Readings*. Englewood Cliffs, N.J., Prentice-Hall, 1991.

Cooper, Robin, et al. *Implementing Activity-Based Cost Management: Moving from Analysis to Action*. Montvale, N.J., Institute of Management Accountants, 1992.

Johnson, H. Thomas. "It's Time to Stop Overselling Activity-Based Cost Management." *Management Accounting*, September 1992, pp. 26-35.

Johnson, H. Thomas, and Robert S. Kaplan. *Relevance Lost: The Rise and Fall of Management Accounting*. Boston, Harvard Business School Press, 1987.

Kaplan, Robert S. "In Defense of Activity-Based Cost Management." *Management Accounting*, November 1992, pp. 58-63.

Pryor, Tom. *Activity Dictionary*. Arlington, Texas, ICMS, Inc., 1992.

Rummler, Geary A., and Alan P. Brache. *Improving Performance: How to Manage the White Space on the Organization Chart*. San Francisco, Jossey-Bass Publishers, 1990.

Turney, Peter B.B. *Common Cents: The ABC Performance Breakthrough*. Hillsboro, Or., Cost Technology, 1992.

Turney, Peter B.B., and Alan J. Stratton. "Using ABC to Support Continuous Improvement." *Management Accounting*, September 1992, pp. 46-50.

A bibliography of books and magazine articles on activity-based costing is available from the library of the Institute of Management Accountants. It is free to members and costs $15.00 for nonmembers. For further information, call the IMA library at (201) 573-6235.

Appendix

A number of PC-based software packages for carrying out activity-based costing are available. Among them are the following:

- *ABC Solutions*. Software Systems, P.O. Box 19208, Indianapolis, IN 46219-0208; (317) 356-3735.

- *Alpha Cost*. VanDeMark Products, 1307 W. Main St. B2-2, Medford, OR 97501; (503) 779-8700.

- *CASSO* (Cost Accounting System for Service Organizations). Automation Consulting, 11500 Hyne Rd., Brighton, MI 48116; (313) 229-2099.

- *CMS-PC*. ICMS Software, Inc., 4025 Woodland Park Blvd., Suite 272, Arlington, TX; (817) 548-9056.

- *Compete!* ManageWare, Inc., 100 First Stamford Pl., Stamford, CT 06902; (203) 359-9397.

- *e^3 System*. Polaris Systems, 1800 Augusta, Suite 216, Houston, TX 77059; (713) 977-3270.

- *Easy ABC*. ABC Technologies, Inc., 8926 S.W. Hall Blvd., Portland, OR 97223; (503) 626-4895.

- *Net Prophet*. Sapling Software Aided Planning Corp., 400 Carlingview Dr., Etobicoke, Ontario, Canada M9W 5X9; (416) 674-8520.

- *Profit Manager, Jr*. Strategic Cost Systems, 80 Woodbine Rd., Belmont, MA 02178; (617) 489-0874.

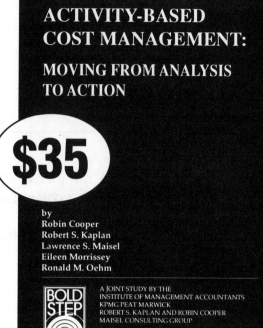

MEMBERSHIP APPLICATION

INSTITUTE OF MANAGEMENT ACCOUNTANTS, INC.

10 PARAGON DRIVE, MONTVALE, NEW JERSEY 07645-1760 • 201-573-9000 • 1-800-638-4427

Check One. (✓) ☐ INITIAL APPLICATION   ☐ REINSTATEMENT

PERSONAL INFORMATION:
(Please Print or Type) Use Black or Blue Ink

Mr. ☐ Ms. ☐ Miss ☐ Mrs. ☐ Dr. ☐ Male ☐ Female ☐ Social Security Number ___ - ___ - ___

First Name   Middle Name   Last Name   First Name or Nickname for IMA Badges (Optional)   Suffix

Professional Designations
☐ CMA   ☐ CPA
☐ CIA   ☐ CFA
OTHER:

Home Street Address   City   State   Zip Code (9 Digit)

Send IMA Mail ☐ Home ☐ Business

Home Telephone Number (   )   Date of Birth ___/___/___   Marital Status (Optional)   Number of Children (Optional)   Year of Birth of Each Child (Optional)

Telephone Preference
☐ Home ☐ Business

Part Time/School Address   Street   City   State   Zip Code (9 Digit)   Telephone Number at Part Time Address (   )   Effective Date (Month to Month)

Spouse's First Name   Middle Name   Last Name   Nickname for IMA Badges   Spouse's Professional Designations

COMPANY NAME: (Please Print or Type)

Hire Date   Telephone Number (   )   Extension   SIC Code (See Reverse Side)   Company Size (Check One)
☐ Under $50 Million
☐ $50-500 Million
☐ $501 Mil-$5 Billion
☐ Over $5 Billion

Street Address   Suite, Room, Mail Stop   Job Title Code (See Reverse Side)

City   State   Zip Code (9 Digit)   Fax Number (   )   Responsibility Code (See Reverse Side)

CHAPTER AFFILIATION: (Name of Chapter/Student Affiliate Chapter/Your Choice)   Chapter Number

Member-At-Large   ☐ Check here if no chapter affiliation desired

EDUCATION - College, Business, Graduate School(s)
(Fill In All Applicable Information)

	MAJOR	DATE(S)	DEGREE(S)

CMA
Certified Management Accountant Program

☐ Check Here to receive information about IMA's prestigious certification program

ADMISSION CRITERIA FOR MEMBERSHIP: INSTITUTE OF MANAGEMENT ACCOUNTANTS, INC. I affirm that I meet the criteria for membership (on reverse side) which I have circled.
Please circle only one. b: 1, 2, 3, 4, 5, 6, 7

CPA Certificate Number   State   Year

Are you required to report CPE hours annually? ☐ No ☐ Yes (See Reverse Side)

Have you ever been convicted of a felony? ☐ No ☐ Yes

MEMBERSHIP - FILL IN AS APPROPRIATE - ALL PAYMENTS MUST BE IN U.S. DOLLARS

DUES

• REGULAR: U.S.A. AND CANADA
☐ 1 Yr. $125 ☐ 2 Yr. $240 ☐ 3 Yr. $345 $ ___

• INTERNATIONAL MEMBER-AT-LARGE $80
You must reside outside the U.S.A. and CANADA

• ACADEMIC: U.S.A. AND CANADA $62.50
Must be a full-time faculty member

• ASSOCIATE: U.S.A. AND CANADA
Must apply within 2 years of completing full-time studies   1st Year $42   2nd Year $83

• STUDENT MEMBERSHIP: U.S.A. AND CANADA $20
Not less than 6 equivalent hours per semester. *Fill in school name below.

*Name of School ___   Expected Date of Degree ___

OPTIONAL SERVICES*
☐ Controllers Council $75
☐ Cost Management Group $75
☐ Research Publication Service $50
**IMA Membership Required

REGISTRATION / REINSTATEMENT FEE
NOTE: Regular, Academic & International Members ONLY

☐ I am enclosing a check payable to: INSTITUTE OF MANAGEMENT ACCOUNTANTS, INC.
☐ Charge my credit card: ☐ VISA ☐ MASTERCARD ☐ AMEX

CREDIT CARD NUMBER ▶   EXPIRATION DATE ▶

$ ___   15 00

$ ___   TOTAL ▶

SIGNATURE X

I affirm the statements on this application are correct and agree to abide by the Standards of Ethical Conduct for Management Accountants.

Sponsor's Name or Signature of Professor or Registrar   Sponsor's Member No. (if applicable)   DATE ___/___/___

PLEASE READ BOTH SIDES   NOTE: PAYMENT IN FULL MUST ACCOMPANY APPLICATION - FEES SCHEDULED TO CHANGE AS OF SEPT. 1, 1993

INSTITUTE OF MANAGEMENT ACCOUNTANTS, INC.

Admission Criteria for Membership - All persons residing within the United States, its possessions, or Canada, and who are otherwise qualified for membership under the Bylaws, are eligible for membership as Regular Members, Associate Members or Student Members as defined in Article II, Section 2, of the Bylaws, provided they meet the following minimum criteria:

(b) (1) Have a full four-year college degree, with a major in accounting or a minimum of 21 semester hours in accounting, or an advanced degree with 15 semester hours in accounting, or

(2) Have a full four-year college degree and hold either a management accounting position or management accounting teaching position or be admitted to the CMA program at the time of admission, or

(3) Have a two-year degree with a minimum of 15 semester hours in accounting plus four years experience in a management accounting position and hold a management accounting position at the time of admission, or

(4) Hold a CMA certificate, a CPA certificate, or their international equivalents, or

(5) Have six years of experience in management accounting, or

(6) Agree to complete 18 Continuing Professional Education (CPE) hours in IMA-approved programs (local or national) in each of the five consecutive years from the date of admission. A member not fulfilling the commitment will automatically be dropped from membership, or

(7) Be a college student carrying a minimum of six undergraduate or graduate hours (or equivalent) per semester within a school, college or university in the United States.

NOTE: Prior felony conviction - This application, with a brief explanation of circumstances, should be sent directly to the Executive Director of IMA at the address on the reverse side of this form in an envelope marked "Confidential".

STANDARD INDUSTRY CLASSIFICATIONS (SIC)

AGRICULTURE, FORESTRY, FISHERIES
01 AGRICULTURAL PRODUCTION
07 AGRICULTURAL SVCS / HUNTING / TRAPPING
08 FORESTRY
09 FISHERIES

MINING
10 METAL MINING
11 ANTHRACITE MINING
12 BITUMINOUS COAL / LIGNITE MINING
13 CRUDE OIL / NATURAL GAS
14 MINING / QUARRYING NONMETALLICS

CONTRACT CONSTRUCTION
15 BLDG. CONSTRUCTION - GENERAL CONTRACTORS
16 CONSTRUCTION - OTHER
17 CONSTRUCTION - SPECIAL TRADE CONTRACTORS

MANUFACTURING
19 ORDINANCE / ACCESSORIES
20 FOOD / KINDRED PRODUCTS
21 TOBACCO MANUFACTURERS
22 TEXTILE MILL PRODUCTS
23 APPAREL / FINISHED FABRICS
24 LUMBER / WOOD PRODUCTS

(MANUFACTURING CONTINUED)
25 FURNITURE / FIXTURES
26 PAPER / ALLIED PRODUCTS
27 PRINTING / PUBLISHING
28 CHEMICALS / ALLIED PRODUCTS
29 OIL REFINING / RELATED INDUSTRIES
30 RUBBER / MISC. PLASTICS PRODUCTS
31 LEATHER PRODUCTS
32 STONE, CLAY, GLASS / CONCRETE PRODUCTS
33 PRIMARY METAL INDUSTRIES
34 FABRICATED METAL PRODUCTS
35 MACHINERY, NONELECTRICAL
36 ELECTRICAL MACHINERY
37 TRANSPORTATION
38 BLDG. CONSTRUCTION, SCIENTIFIC, CONTROL INSTRUMENTS
39 MISC. MANUFACTURING INDUSTRIES

TRANSPORTATION, COMMUNICATION & UTILITY SERVICES
40 RAILROAD TRANSPORTATION
41 LOCAL AND SUBURBAN TRANSPORTATION
42 MOTOR FREIGHT / WAREHOUSING
44 WATER TRANSPORTATION
45 AIR TRANSPORTATION
46 PIPE LINE TRANSPORTATION
47 TRANSPORTATION SERVICES
48 COMMUNICATION
49 ELECTRIC, GAS / SANITARY SERVICES

WHOLESALE & RETAIL TRADE
50 WHOLESALE TRADE
52 BUILDING / HARDWARE / FARM EQUIP DEALERS
53 RETAIL TRADE - GENERAL
54 FOOD STORES
55 AUTO DEALERS / SERVICE STATIONS
56 APPAREL / ACCESSORY STORES
57 FURNITURE / FURNISHINGS / STORES
58 EATING / DRINKING PLACES
59 MISC. RETAIL STORES

FINANCE, INSURANCE & REAL ESTATE
60 BANKING
61 CREDIT AGENCIES NOT BANKS
62 SECURITY / COMMODITY BROKERS, AND SERVICES
63 INSURANCE CARRIERS
64 INSURANCE AGENTS, BROKERS
65 REAL ESTATE
66 COMBINATIONS OF REAL ESTATE, INSURANCE, LOANS, LAW OFFICES
67 HOLDING, INVESTMENT COMPANIES

SERVICES
70 HOTELS / ROOMING HOUSES / CAMPS, ETC.
72 PERSONAL SERVICES
73 MISC. BUSINESS SERVICES
75 AUTO REPAIR, AUTO SERVICES / GARAGES
76 MOTION PICTURES
79 AMUSEMENT / RECREATION SERVICES
80 MEDICAL / HEALTH SERVICES
81 LEGAL SERVICES
82 EDUCATIONAL SERVICES
84 MUSEUM / ART GALLERIES / GARDENS
86 NONPROFIT MEMBERSHIP ORGANIZATIONS
88 PRIVATE HOUSEHOLDS
89 PUBLIC ACCOUNTING

GOVERNMENT
91 FEDERAL GOVERNMENT
92 STATE GOVERNMENT
93 LOCAL GOVERNMENT
94 INTERNATIONAL GOVERNMENT

NONCLASSIFIABLE
99 NONCLASSIFIABLE ESTABLISHMENTS

JOB TITLE
01 OWNER
03 CHAIRMAN OF THE BOARD
05 CHIEF EXECUTIVE OFFICER
06 CHIEF FINANCIAL OFFICER
07 PRESIDENT
09 GROUP PRESIDENT
11 CORPORATE SECRETARY
13 CORPORATE TREASURER
15 EXECUTIVE VICE PRESIDENT
17 SENIOR VICE PRESIDENT
19 VICE PRESIDENT
21 ASSISTANT VICE PRESIDENT
23 GROUP VICE PRESIDENT
25 DIVISIONAL VICE PRESIDENT
27 CORPORATE CONTROLLER
29 ASST. CORPORATE CONTROLLER
31 DIVISIONAL CONTROLLER
33 PLANT CONTROLLER
35 DIRECTOR
37 GENERAL MANAGER
39 MANAGER
41 GENERAL SUPERVISOR
43 SUPERVISOR
45 CHIEF ACCOUNTANT
47 ACCOUNTANT
49 ECONOMIST
51 ANALYST
53 SYSTEMS ANALYST
55 PROGRAMMER
57 ADMINISTRATOR
59 AUDITOR
65 DEAN
67 PROFESSOR
69 ASSOCIATE PROFESSOR
71 ASSISTANT PROFESSOR
73 INSTRUCTOR
75 CONSULTANT
77 PRINCIPAL
79 PARTNER
99 OTHER

RESPONSIBILITY AREA
01 GENERAL MANAGEMENT
05 CORPORATE MANAGEMENT
10 PUBLIC ACCOUNTING
15 GENERAL ACCOUNTING
20 PERSONNEL ACCOUNTING
25 COST ACCOUNTING
30 GOVERNMENTAL ACCOUNTING
35 FINANCE
40 RISK MANAGEMENT
45 BUDGETING AND PLANNING
50 TAXATION
55 INTERNAL AUDITING
60 EDUCATION
65 INFORMATION SYSTEMS
70 STUDENT
75 RETIRED
80 OTHER

Management Accounting subscription rates per year:
• Members $20.00 (included in dues, nondeductible)
• Student Members: $10.00 (included in dues, nondeductible)
• Nonmembers: $125.00
• Nonprofit Libraries: $62.50

Notes

Notes

Notes

Notes

Notes

Notes

Notes

Notes

Notes

Notes

Notes

Notes

Notes

Notes

Notes

Notes